Computers Count

GW00728794

PROFESSIONAL COMMUNICATION

Computers Count

Jaki Howes

RIBA Publications

© Jaki Howes

Published by RIBA Publications Ltd
Finsbury Mission, Moreland Street, London EC1V 8BB

ISBN 0 947877 17 7

Series editor: Alaine Hamilton
Book design: Penny Mills

Typeset by Goodfellow & Egan Ltd, Cambridge
Printed by Billing & Sons Ltd, Worcester

Other publications in this series:
Writing Matters by Alaine Hamilton

Acknowledgements

Contributions to this book are legion and impossible to list in detail. Much of
the information derives from discussions at the Architectural Schools Computing Association conferences and at meetings of the RIBA Computer Committee
and of the Yorkshire Region Information Technology group. Any errors found
in the book are mine.

In particular, I thank Allan McCartney of Databuild Consultants Ltd,
Manchester, and Bob King of the NCC for their factual advice; Julia Clegg for
acting as a professional innocent; my daughter, Jo, for her patience; my
colleagues at Huddersfield Polytechnic for their forbearance; Alaine Hamilton
for constant encouragement, and Les Webb, who thought this book should be
written.

Contents

Foreword

At last, a book about computers, written for architects in language that architects can understand. Computers have made less impact on the practice of architecture than in almost any other field, and there are some very good reasons for this.

Architects tend to be individualists engaged in one-off operations to which the solutions are almost invariably idiosyncratic and seldom crop up a second time, whereas computers are great at following well-trodden paths time and again. Most architects work in small units and cannot afford to develop their own computer solutions – and outside specialists are not keen to do it for them, as architectural work is diverse and is considered an unattractive market, difficult to customise.

Nevertheless, if the profession is to hold its own in an increasingly computerised world, architects simply have to come to grips with the problem. There are many operations in even the smallest practice where the computer can be applied to produce greater accuracy, flexibility and speed. At its most basic level, the word-processor (only another name for a computerised and extremely versatile typewriter) can take the slog out of many of the day-to-day activities.

Computerised accounting may not be the highest priority in most small practices, but a good job-costing system is a must in today's competitive world. Feasibility and viability studies are the bread and butter of work-getting – the 'what if?' facilities of the computer using standard programmes are invaluable. The same standard programmes can aid the control of cashflow and resources, and take much of the headache out of programming. Technical support and computer-aided design may come later but, with the advent of good micro-based systems, computer drafting is rapidly becoming the standard.

Ten years ago, when my own practice took the plunge into computers, there was little help and guidance available. Salesmen talked an unintelligible gibberish, demonstrations were carefully pre-structured to mislead rather than to inform, software was notoriously unreliable and the user was expected to do most of the development work himself. It was a very expensive experience and we still have major reservations on whether it all made commercial sense.

Today, virtually all our accounting and administrative activities are computerised, together with a substantial proportion of our drafting – though by no means all of it. There are still many activities in architecture which are better carried out by the human brain and hand than by a computer.

I read Jaki Howes' book with growing delight. It starts as any good book on this topic must, with the assumption that the reader knows absolutely nothing about computers, and takes him or her through the terminology and the whole process of becoming computerised. It is essential reading, not only for those who are contemplating getting into computers, but for anybody thinking about an upgrade or second generation installation.

The last two words in the book are 'good luck'. The architect who has read all the preceding words and kept the book by him will need a rather smaller ration of that precious commodity than those who haven't.

Ray Cecil
RIBA Vice President, Practice

Preface

Computers count. They add and subtract by counting, they divide by counting, and they multiply by counting. They are machines, no cleverer than the people who use them and certainly not creative or clairvoyant. On the other hand they don't get bored, which means that they can relieve their users of many tedious and complex tasks, which they carry out with great speed and accuracy. Mind you, using a computer can be boring and tedious for humans, and often needs a high degree of concentration.

So do *you* need one? You are certainly interested, or you wouldn't have picked up this book. But do you know what you need to find out so as to make a sensible decision? Or, to put it another way, how do you find out what you need to know?

This book provides some of the answers. It explains in broad terms what computers are, how they work, and what they can do. It gives guidelines for assessing what use a computer would be to you and sets out the questions that you will need to ask yourself and others.

Moving into the computer age requires courage, commonsense and good judgement. It also requires much patient research and evaluation. This book aims to help you to set off in the right direction.

Jaki Howes
August 1989

Introduction

For many people, computers are synonymous with *power*. Sometimes it seems that they are running everything from the supermarket to the Stock Exchange. We know that vast amounts of information, which may affect our health and wealth, are stored in anonymous computers by anonymous people. How safe is it from prying eyes and hacking fingers, we ask ourselves uneasily? Yet at the other end of the scale, schoolchildren easily assimilate computer techniques, play games and write programs happily assuming that when they grow up computers will have grown up too, and be bigger, cleverer and easier to use.

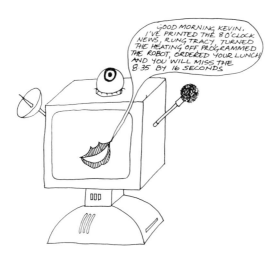

The attitude of the design professions towards the use and acceptance of the available computer technology is ambivalent, to say the least. After all, designers have always seen themselves as having a special skill, an intuitive flair, that can magick a design from nowhere, via a 3B pencil, on to the back of an envelope. To many of them, having to accept that this talent could be taken over by a *machine* would be an intense personal and professional affront. (In any case, it is not possible at present.) On the other hand, most would welcome some obedient

11

machine-generated help and, generally speaking, that is what computers offer: they do precisely what they are told to do – and only that. It's *people* who mess things up.

Given the present range of activities in the design professions, it is generally true to say that where a problem can be defined explicitly, it is possible to write a computer program to solve it. For example, engineering problems involve testing solutions against defined parameters – it is not difficult to accept that this can be done using a computer. Similarly in graphic, surface or textile design, it is easy to see that computers can help the designer to visualise a solution and to experiment with changes of arrangement, pattern or colour without having to redraw each alternative.

In architectural design the success of a solution involves numerous value judgements associated with a building's appearance, structural stability, environmental performance and usability. Because the importance of these criteria varies with each project, the subjective element and the design experience and skill of the architect cannot be eliminated or taken over by a computer nor, given the present state of knowledge, is this likely to happen. This applies, to a greater or lesser extent, to all the design professions.

In all artefact design there are areas of the process in which a computer can be used to advantage, provided that the user has a clear idea of the procedures needed to achieve solutions. The most likely areas are:

Information presentation
(wordprocessing, desktop publishing, drafting, visualisation and animation);
Evaluation of solutions
(mechanical, structural, environmental, spatial, visual, economic);
Organisation and management
(information storage, job costing, flow-charting, accounts).

What the surveys say
Although architecture is behind many other professions in general acceptance of computers, there is a significant growth rate, particularly in large practices and very small practices.

The RIBA Computer Group has run three national surveys. In November 1980, 2,800 questionnaires were sent out and 804 were returned. It was found that 19% of respondents had some kind of computer equipment. In December 1983, questionnaires were sent out to all practices (4,575) and 836 replies were received. This time 309 practices were using a computer – 37% of the response. A third survey was undertaken in 1987: questionnaires were sent out to all practices (about 5,000). Of the 1,927 respondents, 903 had some kind of computer facility (47%), 379 were intending to purchase, and 52 used computer bureaux. However, 373 saw no point in having a computer.

It was no surprise that large practices were the greatest users of computers, nor that all positive respondents were using wordprocessors. The wordprocessor has taken the place of the typewriter to such an extent that it is often forgotten that it is in fact a computer running a program.

About this book
No book can be all things to all people. *Computers Count* aims to help the computer-uninitiated as well as the converted, and each section has been designed to be read in isolation as well as part of the whole discussion. For example, those who already use a computer for wordprocessing and/or administrative purposes but who may be contemplating graphics or drawing applications could move straight from GO to Section 6. However, it's best to begin at the beginning and read on, even though you may encounter some (necessary) repetition.

Checklists are included in many of the sections, and if you are planning a mega upheaval in your office which includes establishing a quality system as well as introducing computer techniques, you may find these particularly relevant. As you will see, they closely resemble the kinds of schedules recommended for quality assurance assessment.

After the main text there is an extensive Glossary for any fallers beside the terminological wayside, although as far as possible explanations are given in the main text as and when they are needed.

As far as currency is concerned, it's impossible to write an up-to-date book about computers, and that is why this one concentrates on general issues and principles and includes only a limited amount of technical information. Other more detailed sources are listed in the Bibliography, but it's important to remember that computers are a moving target: don't rely blindly on the accuracy of published information.

Section 1

What are computers?

You do not need to have an extensive knowledge of the internal workings of a computer or of programming to be able to use applications packages successfully. However, in this case, a little knowledge is not a particularly dangerous thing. A reasonable understanding of the jargon helps when trying not to be blinded by enthusiastic salesmen, who know all the words but may not understand very much more than you about what they mean. Do not be intimidated by 'computerspeak'. If someone cannot explain in plain English, they are possibly stupid, probably ignorant and/or trying to hide something.

1.1 Types of computer

There are two generic types of computer, analogue and digital. This book covers digital computers only, but a simple explanation of the difference may be helpful.

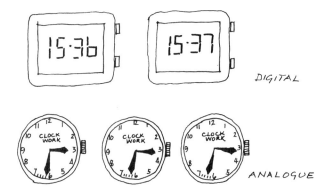

The digital computer represents numbers and other information by discrete states so that it is not possible to move continuously from one value to another; an example of this is the display on a digital watch, which 'jumps' from one value to another. The analogue computer represents numbers and values by physical quantities, such as voltage, which can be measured and which can change continuously – like the position of the hands on a traditional watch. The analogue approach is more difficult in terms of all-purpose computing because analogue computers are always configured to solve a specific problem. Changing the problem is laborious and complex; because of this, commercial software has been developed on the digital computer.

Digital information

Because digital computers operate using discrete states there has to be a method of reducing information to an acceptable code. This is done using the binary system, which enables alphanumeric symbols to be translated to a series of zeros and ones, corresponding electronically to 'off' and 'on'. The binary system represents numbers to base two rather than base ten as in the decimal (or denary) system.

DECIMAL	BINARY
1	0001
2	0010
3	0011
4	0100
8	1000
16	10000
32	100000
64	1000000

Each zero or one is known as a *bit* (Binary digIT). A group of 8 bits (usually) is called a *byte*. A group of 16 bits (up to 64 bits), which forms the 'lump' in which information is handled is known as a *word*.

There are 26 letters in the English alphabet, upper and lower case, 10 numeric symbols, at least 15 punctuation marks and many more special and mathematical symbols, so it can be seen that to represent these discretely, over 100 unique identifiers are required. It takes at least seven bits to do this. When a key is pressed on a keyboard, a code of zeros and ones 8 bits long will be sent to the processor. There is a standard code for doing this which should not vary between different types of machine: the ASCII code (American Standard Code for Information Interchange, pronounced 'Askey'). This consists of 256 unique codes.

Whilst an operator can be fairly sure that the codes for alphanumeric symbols are universal, those for other symbols and function keys are not: they depend on the machine, the keyboard and the software.

What this means, in simple terms, is that keys that look the same do different things on different machines.

Leaving aside these problems and returning to the capabilities of computers, any problem that can be presented in a way which can be reduced to binary code can be handled in accordance with a predetermined program.

1.2 Types of digital computer

Mainframes
These are 'big' computers used by institutions, industry and commerce. They can support a large number of terminals which can be connected directly, by telephone or by satellite links, and allow many simultaneous users. Data is shared. Outside users can sometimes buy time on large systems but this is not now appropriate, except for the interrogation of public data bases, because microcomputer technology has advanced to the state where applications can be supported on small and relatively cheap machines.

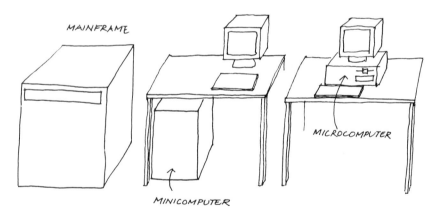

Minicomputers
These are smaller systems which, like mainframes, are capable of supporting multiple general purpose users, and allow data to be shared. At the time of writing the larger and more expensive CAD (computer aided design) software runs on these machines.

Microcomputers
The distinction between 'micro' and 'mini' computers is now (1989)

very woolly (as is the distinction between larger minis and main-frames). The price of a minicomputer has fallen to that of a micro a few years ago. In general, the power of processors is defined by the *word length* (the number of bits handled at one time) but there are other pertinent variables such as the clock speed and the installed operating system. Five years ago microcomputers were 8 bit when minis were 32 bit. The newest generation of 32 bit micros are, in effect, the same as minis, provided an operating system is available which allows multiple use. These 32 bit machines are used in *work stations*, and it it is here that the development of drafting systems is most likely to take place.

The distinction between the three types of digital computer is likely to become meaningless. All you have to worry about is whether a computer has enough memory and is fast enough to handle any applications that you want to use.

Section 2

Hardware

The essential components of a computer system are:

Input devices, which convert information to digital codes (2.1);
A central processor, which handles the data and carries out calculation
and manipulation (2.2);
Back-up storage, devices for storing information when the computer is
switched off)2.3);
Output devices, which convert the result back into an understandable
form (2.4).

All this kit is known as *hardware,* and the parts of it other than the
central processor are known as *peripherals.* The programs or sets of
instructions that tell the hardware how to operate are known as
software. Software that resides inside a machine permanently is *firmware.* In America, but rarely in the United Kingdom, computer
personnel are referred to as *liveware.*

2.1 Input devices

Keyboard
The most common input device is the *keyboard.* This resembles a
typewriter keyboard (QWERTY), but has extra keys for specific purposes. On most keyboards, other than those on home computers, there
is a number pad and a set of function keys which are programmable.

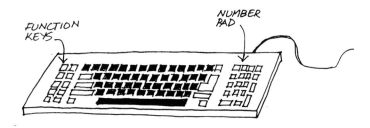

Visual display unit

The *visual display unit* (VDU), which looks like a television screen, is not strictly an input device, but does allow the user to observe the effects of input. VDUs can be monochrome or colour and vary in resolution, that is the number of picture elements (*pixels*) which form the display.

Mouse (mouses, mice, meece – choose your own plural)

A *mouse* is an input device which is about the size of a packet of twenty cigarettes. It has one, two or three buttons at the 'head' end, which have varying functions depending on the breed of mouse, the type of computer and the software being used. It is joined by its very long 'tail' to the processor box. Mice are used to move the cursor on the screen to locate points in drafting systems, to select items from a screen menu, or to select an *icon*. Icons are graphic symbols used instead of words in the screen menus of user-friendly systems.

There are mechanical mice which can be used on a clean, flat surface, and optical mice which are used with a special metal 'mouse-pad'. When a mouse is moved, the cursor changes position on the screen relative to the movement on the pad, and a selection is made by clicking one of the buttons.

Roller balls are 'up-side-down' mice – imagine a cigarette packet with a golf ball in the middle. The cursor is moved by moving the ball.

Graphics tablets and digitisers

Graphics tablets and *digitisers* range in size from A4 to A0. They are electronically 'gridded' so that specific points on them can be determined. They can be used to select options from a menu which is laid out on them or for digitising drawings by locating the beginning and end points of lines and characteristics of curves. Exactly how they operate depends on the particular system. Menu options or points are selected by a *stylus* which is similar to an inkless ballpoint pen, or by a cross-hair cursor (*puck*).

Paddles and joysticks

Paddles and *joysticks* will be familiar to anyone who has played an interactive computer game. They allow the cursor, symbols, monsters and all manner of phantasmagoria to be moved around the screen.

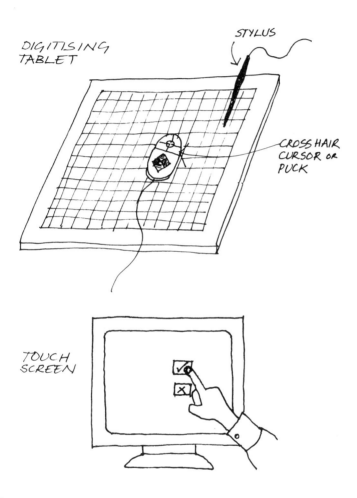

Touch screens

These are currently out of fashion except in the Stock Exchange, where they are enjoying a rebirth. (For limited applications, they are quite simple to use ... .) They allow points to be located on the screen using a light pen, or a menu item to be selected using a light pen or a finger. Difficulties have been experienced involving lack of accuracy, parallax errors, dust, static and damaged screens.

Scanners

Scanners are devices for electronically digitising graphic or photographic material so that it can be handled by a computer, particularly in desktop publishing systems, and reproduced to a specific scale and size by a printer.

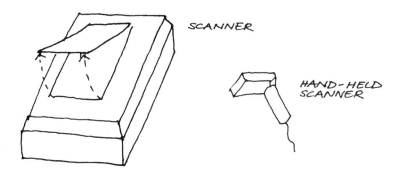

SCANNER

HAND-HELD SCANNER

Voice recognition

There is no doubt that this is a field for development. It is not useful at present in practice applications, but has been used in security systems. As human vocal characteristics vary widely it is difficult to define them unambiguously ('super loan' ... 'soup alone'?) and then to digitise them.

Character recognition

There are developments in the field of character recognition, particularly in converting handwriting to typed text. Here again the immense diversity of characters makes this at present an area for research rather than practical applications.

Input from stored or transmitted data

Input to computers can come from audio, video or magnetic tape, from a floppy, hard or video disk. Data can be transmitted to or received from other computers by telephone link via a *modem* (MOdulator/ DEModulator).

Future developments

Research is progressing, mainly in medical and military circles, to develop input/output devices which can interpret eye, hand and arm movement. These include the *data glove*, which interprets hand movements, and the *data helmet*, which records and translates eye movement. These sophisticated mechanisms are used in flight simulators, so that the operator can observe the direct consequences of his actions. Eventually this technology will percolate into everyday applications.

Developments are under way to make computer interfaces more friendly and easy to use, and input device technology will respond to this.

2.2 Processors

The first electronic computers were developed in the 1940s. These machines were large, slow, filled a whole room, and were operated by valves. In the 1950s, transistors replaced valves. Transistors used less power, generated less heat and took up less space, allowing smaller and more reliable computers to be manufactured.

The greatest advance came in the 1960s with the development of the integrated circuit or *chip*. A chip is a slice of silicon on to which a circuit is photographically copied and then processed. It contains more electronic components than the room-sized computers of forty years ago. Chips with specific roles in the functioning of the computer are mounted on circuit boards. There are many differing types of central processor chips, which determine the computer architecture. The chip, in combination with the clock, determines the speed (measured in megahertz) at which a computer can function.

This is an area into which only the expert should stray. If what goes in and what comes out is acceptable, then the user has no need to know what goes on inside. However as software is developed using specific computer architecture and a specific operating system, it cannot be expected to be portable between different generic types of machine.

The essential elements of a 'computer' – that is, the bit that does the 'thinking' – are the *central processing unit* (CPU), which contains a *control unit* and an *arithmetic and logic unit, random access memory (RAM), read only memory (ROM)*, and a *clock* (a quartz crystal which controls the speed at which the central processor functions). All these components are mounted on a *motherboard*.

The control unit controls the operation of the computer. Input to the processor comes here first and is sent to the correct part of the computer for processing. When this is finished the CPU sends the results to an output device. Processing takes place in the arithmetic and

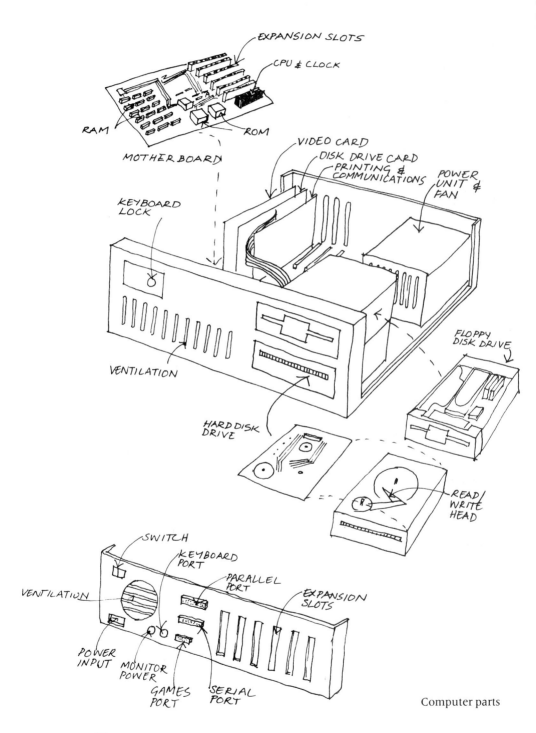

Computer parts

logic unit, whose operations are controlled by sets of instructions in the read only memory (ROM). These instructions are built into the computer and cannot normally be altered.

The other part of the computer's memory, RAM, is the area into which programs for specific applications are loaded and then executed. Computer capacity is often given in numbers of kilobytes or mega-bytes: this refers to the size of RAM, which determines the size of program which can be handled. Software suppliers should state the memory requirements of a program and the desired capacity of the back-up storage. Back-up storage is important because the contents of RAM disappear when the computer is switched off.

2.3 Back-up storage

This is a way of storing information when the computer is switched off. Programs and data can be stored on a variety of media. These storage devices can provide input to or accept output from the CPU.

Punched cards and tape
These used to be used with mainframe computers and are now largely obsolete. They have been superseded by magnetic tape and disks.

Floppy disks and disk drives
Disk drives (mechanisms for reading from and writing to floppy disks) are built nowadays into the body of the computer 'box'. In some older models the disk drive is a separate box.

Floppy disks (diskettes) are made in four main sizes: 3in, 3.5in, 5.25in, and 8in. The two smaller sizes are not 'floppy' at all as they are in a hard plastic case. Some people call them 'stiff' disks. Apart from size there are other variations: disks can be single or double density or single- or double-sided.

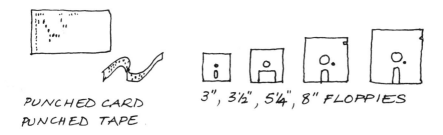

PUNCHED CARD
PUNCHED TAPE

3", 3½", 5¼", 8" FLOPPIES

Before a new disk can be used in a computer it must be formatted for that computer – that is, organised in such a way that it can be read correctly by the read/write head. The likelihood of picking up a disk from one computer and getting it to operate properly on a different type of machine is slight. Even if the machines are meant to be compatible there are often variations.

Floppy disks vary in storage capacity from 250 to 700 kilobytes. A single-spaced sheet of A4 paper contains about 3 kbytes of data; therefore one 300 kbyte floppy can store about 100 pages of information. Disks full of data soon mount up and have to be indexed and stored safely.

Hard (Winchester) disks
A hard disk may be built into the body of the computer. The storage capacity is generally between 10 and 70 megabytes (million bytes). Programs that are used frequently can be stored on the hard disk, which is very much faster than mounting them from floppies each time they are to be used. Hard disks are essential for some programs and are invariably used for drafting systems.

The hard disk drive may or may not be visible from the outside of the computer box, but there should be a warning light to show when it is working. Drives are conventionally named A, B (floppy) and C (hard). Data on a hard disk can be lost or corrupted if an operator mistakenly thinks that he or she is formatting a floppy disk in drive C.

Tape streamers
These are used as a fast method for making back-up copies from a hard disk. A tape streamer is another 'box', which operates in a similar way to a tape recorder. It has to be connected to the computer.

Laser disks
These are high capacity disks which need to be read by a laser beam. They are expensive at present, and not in general office use. A laser disk can store twice the amount of information contained in the *Encyclopaedia Britannica*.

Cassette tapes
Cassette tapes, which are more or less the same as audio tapes, are used in home computers. They are much too slow for business and commercial use.

2.4 Output devices

Visual Display Units

VDUs can be colour or monochrome and are available in much the same sizes as television screens. There are several different types of VDU, but those associated with microcomputers are commonly *raster*, a type of screen display when the screen is scanned many times per second (like a TV screen). The 'picture' on the screen is made up by numbers of dots or 'picture elements', *pixels*. The greater the number of pixels, the greater the screen resolution. A screen which has acceptable resolution for text may be inadequate for linework.

Whilst a low resolution monochrome screen may be adequate for infrequent use, it is totally inappropriate where an operator has to sit in front of it all day for, say, wordprocessing or drafting. The higher the resolution, the higher the memory requirements for the system, and therefore the higher the cost. Colour and high resolution are recommended for graphics and drafting.

Printers

Printers are the most commonly used device for producing hard copy from the output of computers. It must be remembered that if this output is to be used for business purposes, the quality will ultimately depend on the printer and not on the level of sophistication of the computer and the software.

There are numerous types of printer, and their characteristics can vary in four major ways:

the order in which data is printed. Data can be printed one character, one line or one page at a time. In general the more that is printed, the faster the printer;

the way in which data is printed. Characters can either be printed by the impact of a printing head on the paper, or by the non-impact transfer of the printing medium to paper (impact printers are noisy);

how characters are formed. Characters can be made up of dots selected from a regular matrix or by the impact of a solid (metal or plastic) font (similar to those used on typewriters);

how data is sent to the printer. Data is sent to a printer either one bit at a time (that is, *serially*) or one character at a time up to 10 bits (that is, *in parallel*). Generally parallel printers are faster.

Printers vary in speed, quality of output, noisiness and cost. The four main types that are currently used with microcomputers are dot matrix, ink jet, daisy wheel, and laser.

DOT MATRIX (impact, thermal and thermal transfer)
Dot matrix printers form characters from a series of dots. These are produced by a printing head from which different sets of pins are pushed forward to strike an inked ribbon. These printers have been relatively cheap and rather noisy, and until recently did not produce letter quality output. There are now more complex and quieter versions with a greater number of pins, which operate by the transfer of ink from a ribbon either electrostatically or thermally. The text output quality is good and graphics can be produced.

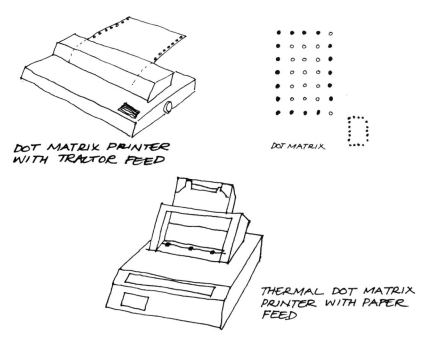

DOT MATRIX PRINTER
WITH TRACTOR FEED

DOT MATRIX

THERMAL DOT MATRIX
PRINTER WITH PAPER
FEED

Thermal printers are non-impact dot matrix printers which are low cost and sometimes supplied packaged with personal computers. Selected needles from a matrix are heated and form a pattern of dots on heat-sensitive paper. Whilst they are cheap to buy and almost silent, they are unsuitable for most business uses because of high running costs and because they need special paper. This makes them less versatile in use.

DAISY WHEEL

Daisy wheel printers are so called because they produce characters from the impact on a ribbon of a printing head which has one character on each 'spoke' of a rotating 'wheel' which resembles the petals of a daisy. Similar mechanisms can be seen on some typewriters. These printers, although noisy and relatively expensive, have been considered until recently to be the only type capable of producing letter-quality output at a reasonable cost. (But note that they cannot produce graphics.) Now dot matrix printers are available at approximately the same cost which can produce equivalent quality text with the addition of graphics. Superior quality text and graphics can be achieved (at two to three times the cost) using a laser printer. Exit daisy wheel?

DAISY WHEEL

INK JET PRINTER
WITH TRACTOR FEED

INK JET

These printers are less popular than dot matrix and daisy wheel types. They are non-impact and consequently quiet. Droplets of ionised ink are 'fired' at the paper. Not only can these printers produce reasonable quality output, both text and graphics, but with enough jets and ink supplies they can produce colour.

Their disadvantage is that if they are not used frequently the jets can clog up and for monochrome text they are no better than cheaper machines. The quality of colour work depends on what the software can drive, and cost for cost this is not as efficient as other printing methods.

A recent development is the bubble printer, which uses precise ink jets directed through electronically controlled hypodermic needle-like pins. These are claimed to produce superior colour rendering.

LASER PRINTERS

The current 'state-of-the-art!' These are printers which use a laser and magnetised ink to produce an image of a complete page. They are fast and silent. Line drawings, graphics work and photographs can be reproduced provided that suitable hardware and software are available. A wide range of fonts, points and heights for text can be produced. The output is almost as good as that achieved by typesetting.

It is difficult to predict whether these printers will become the norm. The price has fallen dramatically and by the time this book is published it may be that the versatility and obvious advantages will outweigh any extra cost – but there may be other developments.

Printers should be selected for the match between their capabilities and the required output, their compatibility with the computer and the software, their speed, robustness and cost.

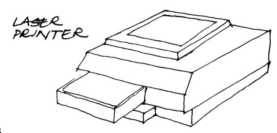

Plotters

Plotters are expensive and can cost as much as the total of the software and other hardware for a micro-based drafting system. Plotters produce line drawings which, according to the complexity of the plotter, can have varying line colours, styles and thicknesses, and a range of fonts.

FLAT BED

These vary in size from A4 to A0. The paper is laid flat and anything from one to eight pens travel over the paper. With appropriate software different line colours and thicknesses can be produced.

DRUM

In drum plotters the paper moves backwards and forwards over a drum and a number of pens move from side to side. The paper can either be fed sheet by sheet or from a continuous roll. Drum plotters take up less horizontal area than flat bed plotters. Obviously, output that requires a drawing to be carried out with a single pen is simpler than output that carries instructions about line style, width and colour and requires

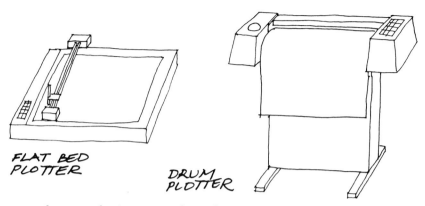

FLAT BED PLOTTER

DRUM PLOTTER

several pens. Plotting can take a long time (literally hours) and is usually carried out 'off-line'. Plotting time increases with complexity.

Pen plotters tend to be favoured for architectural drawings as they are similar in style to those produced manually (but they are much more accurate).

Quality of output often depends on the condition of the equipment rather than its capabilities. Paper-feeds jam and pens get worn, run out and misbehave in a similar way to other drawing pens. The alternative is to use electrostatic plotters, which operate in a similar way to photocopiers. These are at present inordinately expensive and are not in common use.

Other output devices

Voice simulation, music synthesisers, and robotics are all currently being developed, but have as yet little relevance in practice.

Enough about hardware for the time being! Let's suppose you have come by a computer (central processor and memory) and peripherals (input and output devices). What happens when you switch on?

Not much, apparently. There you sit in front of the VDU and all you see is a little cursor blinking at you expectantly or an icon that has a distinctly vacuous stare. 'What are they waiting for?', you mutter irritably. Well, unless the manual for the hardware has a tutorial section on programming from scratch or unless you have some software, you and the computer are going to blink at each other until the machine suffers from power failure or you from terminal boredom. A computer without software is a collection of useless electronic junk.

The point of course being that computers are essentially 'empty'. They require a program of instructions to tell them what to do, ie *software*.

Section 3

Software

Software can be divided into three types:

System software, which controls how the computer runs (3.1);
Programming languages, which allow logical problems to be converted to a format which can be 'understood' by a computer (3.2);
Applications software (packages), which allow a user to carry out specific tasks (3.3).

3.1 System software

Control programs
Control programs determine the operation of the hardware. These programs are written in machine code and are used by the operating system to control how the computer functions. Generally control programs are built into the computer, in ROM, and are known as *firmware*.

Operating systems
An operating system is a program or programs designed to control how the computer operates, the transfer of data to and from peripheral devices, the order in which tasks are executed, locations in RAM, the management of tasks and the flow of data. Operating systems are manipulated internally by means of a job control language, which is machine specific. Operating systems are developed using assembly languages which are symbolic codes used to represent machine code instructions.

At the time of writing there are several common operating systems, including MS-DOS (produced by the Microsoft Corporation), PC-DOS (the IBM version of MS-DOS), Multifinder (Apple's multi-tasking system), CP/M, and UNIX. The capabilities of these systems differ, and so does their mode of operation, protocol and screen messages. The micro-channel computer architecture which is being developed by IBM will require a new operating system (OS/2). If this catches on it will supersede machines which operate like the IBM-PC. This diversity does not make life easy for the computer user who is not a 'buff'. Programs written for use on one operating system are not likely to run on another, nor can operating systems be instantly transferred to run on any particular generic type of computer.

In an ideal user-friendly world the user should not be aware of the operating system. The installation should have been done by the supplier, screen instructions and manuals should be explicit and unambiguous and the user should just be able to get on with it. Would that life were so simple!

If a computer has been well set up (and this can only be done by someone with an extensive knowledge of the operating system) with a clear opening menu and sets of options and instructions, the user should have little difficulty – until something goes wrong. It is not unusual to strike an incorrect combination of keys, meet a *bug* (a recurring fault that makes nasty things happen) in a program, or run out of space on a disk. It is essential, even with an installed software package, for at least one person in a practice to have a working knowledge of the operating system and be able to manipulate files and to load programs.

3.2 Programming languages

Applications software is written in high level languages which correspond more closely to English than do assembly languages or machine codes. For instance, the English-like instructions PRINT, GOTO, and WRITELN represent a complex set of instructions in machine code. High level languages are converted to machine code either by a *compiler* or by an *interpreter*. A compiler translates the program all at once and and produces an executable application; an interpreter translates line by line during operation. Some of the commonly used programming languages are:

BASIC (Beginner's All-purpose Symbolic Instruction Code)
FORTRAN (FORmula TRANslator)
PASCAL (named after Blaise Pascal)
COBOL (COmmon Business Oriented Language)
C (named by Bell Laboratories – followed language B)

Each language has its own rules, syntax and grammar, and is more suitable for some applications than others. COBOL is used for business applications, FORTRAN for scientific, C with UNIX operating systems, and BASIC is the most widely used general purpose language for microcomputers. It is relatively easy to learn compared with the others, but even so it takes several months to become reasonably proficient. *Don't panic!* You don't need any knowledge of programming to be able to use applications software and packages.

3.3 Applications software

Applications software is developed to carry out specific tasks, for instance structural and environmental calculations. It is written in programming or assembly languages, but this is only of passing interest to the user, who should be able to run the program provided the instructions are carried out accurately and in the right sequence.

Programs can be supplied in source code (the programming language), which allows the user to modify the program (not for beginners!), or in object code, a compiled version in machine language. Object code programs take up less memory but cannot be altered.

However clever and sophisticated the internal workings of software, its value lies in how easy it is to use. There is far too much elegant software produced that takes an age to learn to use, is unforgiving when a mistake is made, and is poorly and insufficiently documented. The importance of ease of use cannot be over-emphasised. It is essential that mistakes can be corrected without having to abort a program or having to jump to the beginning of a routine. Help facilities are often provided on screen, and should be clear. Often, alas, they are not. If users don't know *what* mistake they have made, the help facilities may be useless.

Always check the documentation for the equivalent of a 'what to do in emergencies' section of a car handbook. Software producers often assume, erroneously, that the user has a innate knowledge of the operating system and will be unlikely to leave out some fundamental procedure.

Packages
Packaged software is produced for specific applications and is suitable for a wide range of users − a set of universal tools! Packages are available which include, for example, combinations of wordprocessing, spreadsheets, databases and graphics. They are usually protected, compiled into object code and therefore machine specific, although

there may be an install program which allows them to be used on a range of hardware. Packages are generally user-friendly, using commands which are close to natural language. There is an increasing use of menu-, window- and icon-driven packages where the user selects an option from the screen using a mouse and only data is input from the keyboard.

The success of a package depends on how well it is documented. A user is not interested in the internal structure provided it works. A poorly internally structured program which nevertheless works, is well-documented and easy to use is greatly preferable to a highly sophisticated, all-singing, all-dancing program, which is unforgiving, complicated and poorly documented – and therefore useless.

3.4 Software development

Whether software is developed in-house by a programmer or consultant or as a package, there are five procedural steps:

- the task must be defined and a protocol for carrying it out established. This can be done either by the potential user or by a systems analyst;
- the logical steps for carrying out the task as defined must be established;
- the logical steps have to be converted to a program by coding in a programming language;
- the program must be run, checked for errors, and amended to include screen messages that make it as easy to use as possible;
- documentation must be prepared so that other people can use the program.

The computer user can carry out some or all of these stages, but the second onwards would normally be undertaken by systems analysts or programmers. It is essential that the task is defined clearly by the user. You must know specifically what you would like a program to be able to do – it may not be possible, but at least an objective is defined.

In general terms it is unrealistic to develop software in-house except for clearly defined mathematical models, and even then it is not worth re-inventing the wheel. For instance, a steady state heat loss calculation is easy to program in BASIC, provided that the associated data is held in manual records. It has been done many times before and programs are available with built-in data for the properties of different materials. The time involved in preparing a similar program would cost more than buying an off-the-peg version.

If after investigation it appears that programs are not available for a particular application, then there are three options:

- employ a consultant or software house to produce some;
- take the closest fit existing software and have it customised. This is not easy and often impossible;
- re-examine the need for the application and consider a change of procedure.

The first two options will be expensive but, if the application is considered essential, may prove cost-effective.

Devise an acceptance test for software, a benchmark for performance. Do not pay for software unless it meets the benchmark. It is unwise for inexperienced or first-time users to get involved at this level: they should adopt a fourth option – forget it! It is far wiser to acquire some experience on a well- tried and reliable package which will be useful now, and then consider more ambitious developments when you are more familiar with computers and their terminology.

Obviously the choice of software depends on the user's knowledge, experience and the type of application required, but for new users it is essential that the task is defined and the software selected before any hardware is purchased.

Do not buy a computer and then look for something for it to do. You may find yourself with software you have been persuaded to buy for your machine which doesn't quite work. Many offices have substantial libraries of *shelfware* – software which has been bought, never used properly, and forgotten.

3.5 Applications – an overview

Computer applications in offices fall broadly into five categories:

Presentation:
wordprocessing, desktop publishing, (drafting) graphics and paint;
Information storage and retrieval:
databases and file-handling systems;
Management:
spreadsheets and predictive modellers;
Design aids:
visualisation, drafting, modelling, structural and environmental calculations.

The fifth category is *Communications*, the transfer of data to remote computers. This is *electronic* communication, not to be confused with the administrative applications referred to in this section. Communications software is reviewed in 6.6.

Drafting is included in design aids because, although it is strictly a medium for presentation, it is closely associated with visualisation and modelling.

A simple description will be given of each application to give an overview; more detail is given in Section 6.

Presentation

WORDPROCESSING (see also 6.1)

At its simplest a wordprocessor is like a very forgiving typewriter. Secretaries who have approached the new technology with some apprehension have been swiftly seduced by the capabilities of the machine — gone are the days of liquid correction fluid and carbon copies! A good touch-typist can work much faster than on an electric typewriter and with greater accuracy. Mistakes can be corrected, lines and paragraphs inserted. A one-fingered typist can be just as accurate but it all takes somewhat longer!

Two architects were overheard at the Construction Industry Computer Fair in 1988.

'What do you make of this computer business? I haven't got one — have you?'

'No, I don't see the point ... but I've had a wordprocessor for years.'

Such is the widespread use of wordprocessors that they are not considered to be computers. Strictly they are not — a wordprocessor is a piece of software that runs on a computer.

There are wordprocessing packages available for every make of computer and quite often a package is supplied with the hardware. There are about five market leaders at present, some of them more suitable than others for specific applications, so when making a choice it is essential to ensure that a package can produce, easily, the standard office documentation.

Wordprocessors can store standard documents that can be amended to suit a particular job and then stored on a disk relating to that job. This means that, for example, standard letters can be kept on disk. If the wordprocessor is linked to a database, containing names and addresses, a complete mail shot can be generated. (Most printers do not like addressing envelopes, so either sheets of labels have to be printed or envelopes with windows have to be used.)

Standard specifications can be obtained on disk, or if a practice uses its own specification this can be typed once and stored. In either case clauses can be added, deleted or amended without a complete retype.

Reports and documents can be typed in draft, printed out for manual correction, and then easily amended.

Wordprocessors can justify text right and left, centre it, tabulate, indent and produce bold type. The quality of the printed output depends mainly on the printer, which should be chosen with care. Printers can produce letter quality (and better) text and some can produce colour and graphics. It is important to match the office requirements for quality of documentation with the capabilities of the wordprocessor and printer combination.

DESKTOP PUBLISHING (see also 6.2)
Desktop publishing (DTP) is a cross between typesetting (whose jargon it has adopted) and wordprocessing (of which it is an extension). It has increased in popularity as the price of laser printers has fallen, although they are not essential unless near typeset quality is required.

DTP systems allow text, drawings and photographs to be 'pasted up' page by page into a variety of standard formats. The text quality is not as good as typesetting (currently a resolution of 300 rather than 1,200 dots per inch) but may be acceptable for most everyday purposes. There are a range of fonts, points and sizes. Drawings that have been produced on drafting and graphics systems can be transferred with varying ease; text files and output from some wordprocessors can be input directly, and images can be input from a scanner, or from a graphics or paint package.

These systems are difficult to justify in an architect's office unless a large quantity of illustrated reports, brochures and promotional material needs to be produced in-house; and only then if the output from the DTP is of adequate quality for reproduction or is in sufficient quantity to use for page proofs for subsequent typesetting.

A DTP system can be mounted on an existing computer provided it has sufficient capacity, but additional hardware may be required, for example a scanner and a laser printer.

DRAFTING, GRAPHICS AND PAINT SOFTWARE (see also 6.5, 6.7)
Drafting systems enable the designer to simulate the functions of a set-square, T-square, ruler, pen and drawing board on the computer.

Graphics systems allow the simulation of various means of free-hand and technical drawing. They are less exact in terms of representation of a scaled-down model of a 'real object', but often more versatile in their ability to create variations of two-dimensional pattern and texture. Paint software allows colour to be added to graphic images.

Information storage and retrieval

FILERS, DATABASES AND FILE HANDLING SYSTEMS (see also 6.4)
Filers are systems that allow some interaction between files and also for searching within files. They are not strictly databases but look similar to the non-expert. In most cases these systems prove adequate for the storage of records in practice.

A database is an electronic card index or filing cabinet but is much more versatile than either (except you can't hide the malt whisky or a spare pair of tights in a database). Databases vary in size according to the software and the capacity of the computer, from the equivalent of a card index to that of a public library.

The advantage of using a database rather than a manual system is the facility for cross-referencing and searching files. For instance a database could contain the names, addresses and particulars of all the consultants, contractors, suppliers and clients associated with a practice. It could then be searched for 'people called Brown', 'people called Brown who are contractors' or for 'people called Brown who are contractors based in Epping' and so on. The number of fields that can be searched and the complexity of the cross-referencing depends on the sophistication (and therefore generally the cost) of the software.

Databases can be used in conjunction with other types of software, particularly with spreadsheets in management packages.

A database that is incomplete is useless. It is an exacting and time-consuming task to keep an in-house database up to date.

Another problem is the confidentiality of stored information. ('Who has the key to the drawer that has the key to the safe?') This applies equally to databases. It is possible to protect all or sections of the information by a series of passwords, and the number of levels of access should be considered before the system is set up. A skilful locksmith can get into a safe or if desperate can blow it. A dedicated hacker can find the way into a computer system a lot more quietly, given enough time and privacy. Computer-stored information is more prone to accidental and malicious damage than information stored by conventional methods.

PUBLIC DATABASES AND LIBRARIES

A large amount of information is held on public databases which can be accessed by an individual using a computer, a modem and a telephone link. The user may pay a subscription to the database manager and will pay for connect-time. In addition there is the payment to British Telecom for the use of the line. The whole process can be very costly and the quality and speed of information retrieval varies.

To date very few architects use this type of facility and most have either found the service inadequate or not cost-effective. Maybe there will be improvements in the future. The Building Research Establishment has a directory of databases, and will give information about costs. There are also agencies, including BRE, who will carry out a computer search for a one-off charge. The range of information includes BRE and BSIRA digests, technical information, product data and Acts of Parliament.

Management (see also 6.9)

This is an area where it may be difficult to fit a computer system into existing work methods. In the changing professional climate, architectural practices must know what they do and how they do it in order to survive in a highly competitive and increasingly commercial market. A more businesslike philosophy may mean changes in the quality of documentation and presentation, communications standards, types of drawings, design co-ordination, accounts, project management and office organisation.

Architects traditionally do not like to think of themselves as sales or business people, but that is what they will have to become, whilst retaining their professional skills and integrity, if they are to remain co-ordinators and leaders of the design team.

There is software available for accounting, cash flow, payroll, timesheets and other financial applications. Although computers are mindless, they are exacting: they require their users to be accurate. If your accounting procedures are haphazard, non-existent or in a mess, they will need sorting out before you embark on a search for software to help establish a more efficient regime. There is no point in trying to fit a woolly domestic accounting system into a smart computerised system. In such a case it would be sensible to find out what financial or general models the systems use before setting about revising your office procedures.

Job management and costing systems are excellent for 'what ifs'. These systems allow for the period ahead to be planned and staff time allocated, either for the office as a whole or job by job. The timescale can be input together with the projected fee income, the number of staff involved on each job, staff salaries and other pertinent information.

The effects of delays, changes in salaries or staffing or the advent of a new job can be assessed. Some of these packages can be linked to accounting, database or wordprocessing packages. There is some flexibility in how a package can be set up to suit an individual practice but, as with accounting packages, it may be necessary to alter existing office practice to make a computer application appropriate. There is nothing to be gained by changing an existing efficient system; if there is no obvious computerised replacement it is a better policy to wait, and keep an eye on developments.

Some general office management packages are based on a combination of wordprocessing, database and spreadsheet software. These give versatile prediction tools for a variety of applications, including management, accounting and payroll.

SPREADSHEETS (see also 6.3)
Conceptually a spreadsheet is a large sheet of paper ruled out into rows and columns. In computer terms the paper is the available memory of the computer, and the grid can be displayed on the screen as a series of rows and columns.

The rows are numbered from 1 to whatever, and the columns A–Z and so on, depending on the size of the sheet. Each location is defined by column and row, and is known as a *cell*. Each cell is capable of containing a series of characters or a variable. To give a very simple example of how a spreadsheet operates, suppose a number were entered in A1, and a second number in B1. By entering the formula (A1+B1) in C1, the sum of the two numbers would be displayed in cell C1. If the number in either A1 or B1 were changed, the result in C1 would also change.

Because a spreadsheet can accept characters or numeric data, complicated models can be set up where some cells are used to label others, data formulae and variables entered and the results of changes seen instantly. Spreadsheets can also be used either to observe the effects of 'what ifs' or to carry out straightforward calculations. They are used as the basis of a number of office and job management systems, but can also be used to hold formulae and demonstrate the

42

effects of changing variables in structural and environmental calculations.

PROJECT MANAGEMENT (see also 6.10)
There are a number of project management systems that are based on critical path analysis of the type commonly used by contractors. Those which have been developed for use by architects may be linked to cost control or other management systems.

Design aids

DRAFTING SYSTEMS (see also 6.7)
Drafting systems draw – in two dimensions. They do not hold a model of a building or artefact but a record of lines, curves and points – that is, a drawing. The major difference between computer-generated drawings and those produced manually is that computer drawings are exact. This means that the days of the bodger are limited: input has to be exact. In fact, some general purpose systems are *too* exact for architectural use. Architectural drawings vary in scale from 1:2500 to 1:1, so that working to a possible accuracy of 0.01mm is difficult.

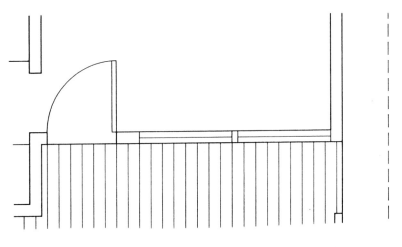

TYPICAL OUTPUT FROM A DRAFTING SYSTEM
(VERSACAD)

It takes roughly the same amount of time to input a computer drawing as it does to draw it by hand, but it is after this that the advantages of a drafting system become apparent. The whole or parts of the drawing can be produced to any size or scale, and can be mirrored, copied, rotated, hatched or automatically dimensioned. Annotation is added by means of a keyboard; it is of a consistent standard and can be done much more quickly than any other method.

Drawing systems have a number of *layers* (known variously, depending on the system, as *views, levels* or *overlays*) which can be imagined as sheets of tracing paper. This means, for instance, that a basic plan showing spatial arrangement can be shown on one layer, furniture layouts can then be drawn 'over' it on another layer and a services layout on a third. These layers can be put together in combinations which provide the relevant amount of information for a specific purpose. A part of a drawing may be increased in scale and automatically 'traced' to another layer where further detail can be added. There is a limit to the number of layers on each system, and some allow for the use of only one colour per layer. What else the system can do depends on the particular system.

The major advantage of any drafting system is the ease with which alterations can be made to a drawing or set of drawings. (No more erasers and razor blades!) Records of each amendment can be kept on disk if necessary or just the most up to date version.

Drafting systems are appropriate where a practice uses standard details or is involved in schemes with a large number of repetitive units, such as housing, hospitals, industrial buildings etc.

'2½D SYSTEMS'

This is a term that has been used for drafting systems which, if heights are input, have the capability of generating elevations, isometric or axonometric projections and sometimes perspectives. The system is not generating these drawings from a 3D model of the building, but from one drawing to another, in much the same way as it would be done by manual methods, but much faster. The term is becoming obsolete, because the demand for even rudimentary '3D' drawings has been such that most drafting systems include these facilities.

Some of the large 'modelling' systems which run on minicomputers have developed from drafting systems with add-on-goodies rather than from true models.

Do you need a drafting system?

This might be better stated as 'can you afford to have or not to have a drafting system?' If the practice has a wide variety of one-off jobs which vary in size, and if it can cope quite well with the existing staff, employing contract draughtsmen if necessary, a drafting system is not going to be a lot of help. Of course, if the computer is there as a status symbol to convince potential clients that the practice is 'thoroughly modern', and if the capital is available, there may be a range of jobs which will benefit from the application of a system. (Particularly if a large number of changes during the contract period can be foreseen.) Many practices do not use their computers half as much as they would like people to think they do!

A small system can be very cheap, but there are limits to what size of scheme can be handled. This may depend on the software itself, or on the amount of space available on a disk.

Starting from scratch, a reasonably versatile system will cost, at 1989 prices:

	£
Computer	2,000
High resolution colour monitor	1,800
Software	2,500
Digitising tablet	600
A3 plotter (7,500 A1 plotter)	1,500
Total	8,300

+ 15% pa for hardware maintenance
+ 15% pa for software maintenance
+ £1000 pa for stationery, disks and running costs
+ depreciation (write off after five years)
+ training costs and time
+ increase in salary for personnel using system
+ extra office space, furniture, equipment and wiring.

If a very small practice (one or two architects) invests in a single computer it could be used to run several applications, including a drafting system, provided that only one or two people use the system. It is unwise to interrupt one application with another. Apart from the time wasted, the risk of making mistakes and losing data is increased. To be efficient and cost-effective a drafting station should be used for that purpose all the time; it should be thought of and used as a drawing board.

With a single station early decisions must be made about which jobs go through the computer and which do not. It is often an advantage to produce design drawings manually and then develop a set of production drawings on the computer; these can then be amended and cross-referenced with greater ease and accuracy than is possible by hand. Remember that with a single station, drafting and plotting cannot be carried out simultaneously (unless there is a plotter buffer), and time must be allowed for plotting. This can take about an hour for a moderately complex working drawing.

Larger mini-based drafting systems can support several terminals, that is several simultaneous users who may not be working on the same job. These systems are generally more sophisticated and have greater capabilities than those that run on micros, and are consequently a lot more expensive. There is a growing use of 'work stations' which are based on 32-bit micros. These will also support more than one user, and are relatively expensive. These systems can be justified if the practice is involved in the design of complex schemes in which there is a large amount of repetition either of building types, room types or details.

It is difficult to estimate the profitability of these 'larger' drafting systems: several attempts have been made, but clearly what is true for one office need not necessarily be true for another. There should, however, be a significant improvement in the quality, consistency and accuracy of drawings. Many drafting systems now have some visualisation capabilities which are useful at the design stage.

MODELLING SYSTEMS (see also 6.7)
There is some confusion about what is meant by a modelling system. Wire-line and surface modelling can be considered as visualisation aids, whilst solid modelling, used in its true sense, is largely an engineering application which allows objects to be created in three dimensions and attributes assigned to them. A true solid modelling system would allow a model to be created which would behave as an analogue of a physical object.

WIRE-LINE MODELS These are created by locating points in three-dimensional space and joining them up with lines or curves that represent edges. The object or building can then be viewed from any angle or height and in perspective. The most basic wire-line modellers are not expensive and can be invaluable in the early stages of design for comparing solutions, especially in terms of massing. Some modellers will allow hidden lines to be removed, which makes the drawing easier to read. Output is often used to form a basis for design perspectives; however, these modellers are not drafting systems and cannot be used as such.

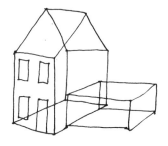 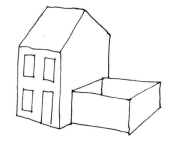

WIRE-LINE MODEL   WIRE-LINE WITH HIDDEN LINES REMOVED

SURFACE MODELLERS   These model objects as a series of infinitely thin planes. The planes can be generated by joining points on lines, curves or splines. Surface modellers are used most commonly in engineering (for instance to visualise car bodies), and in product design and advertising. Their architectural application is limited to exterior and interior perspectives and terrain modelling.

These models can be coloured, shaded, and shadows can be generated. In sophisticated systems more than one light source can be accommodated by means of ray-tracing. As these models have no 'substance', architectural drawings tend to look a bit cardboardy unless great care is taken with the definition of planes.

SURFACE MODEL

SOLID MODELLERS   In solid modellers geometric solids are created as 'lumps of stuff', which can be rotated, sectioned or viewed from any angle. Whereas in a surface model there is nothing in the middle of

what appears to be a solid, in this case there is! What it is can be
defined by the assignation of a series of attributes, based on mathematical models. Calculations can then be carried out for such properties as
centre of gravity, mass, weight and inertia. The most widespread use of
these modellers is in the design of engineering components.

The application becomes complicated in architectural terms. Buildings are hollow, but the components of which they are made are not.
In order to construct a full solid model of a building, the exact size,
configuration and properties would have to be known for every
component. Either there would have to be a definitive set of drawings
or the designer would have to carry a full three-dimensional model in
his head. Architects do not normally work to this degree of exactitude.
Taken to the limit a three-dimensional architectural modelling system
would have to be the equivalent of programmable 'intelligent Lego'.

SOLID MODEL

INTEGRATED DESIGN SYSTEMS

There are several existing systems for architectural use that are
marketed as 'modelling' systems. These are usually an amalgam of
drafting system, database and modeller. It does not really matter to the
user how the system works provided that it does what it sets out to do.
These systems can appear to have the characteristics of a solid or
surface modeller and at the same time allow for the assignation of
attributes to components and complex calculations to be carried out.
The complexity of the systems makes them expensive, difficult to learn
and even more difficult to use to their full capacity.

This is the area where development will take place rapidly. It is clear
that if a computer-generated 'prototype' building could be produced
before it was built, it could be tested thoroughly. Computers cannot
function accurately without complete information, so in order to
produce such a system, dynamic databases of all building information,
including products and their properties, would have to be developed
and, on top of this, the designer would have to be able to define all the

geometric and physical characteristics of a building and its location. If this becomes possible, all structural, environmental and financial calculations could be carried out and the 'finished' building could be viewed internally or externally from any angle. The system could be fully integrated so that the implications of any change could be assessed immediately.

At present (1989) the top end of the range of integrated design systems provides series of linked modules which allow specific functions to be carried out – for instance ground modelling linked to building modelling, both linked to a general drafting system and an interactive database. A range of calculations can be carried out and the range will have increased by the time you read this. Although these systems are expensive (five noughts) most major companies have introduced low cost micro-based entry systems which can be used for familiarisation and can sometimes be upgraded as required.

STRUCTURAL AND ENVIRONMENTAL CALCULATIONS (see also 6.8)
There is some doubt about the advisability of architects carrying out their own calculations, especially as indemnity premiums rise. On the other hand, for small practices who do not normally work with consultants there are structural and environmental calculation packages from which the output is acceptable to Building Control in lieu of 'hand made' calculations. Before buying any program for this purpose, it is advisable to check its acceptability with the local authority.

In a multi-disciplinary practice computers are likely to be used already for carrying out routine calculations. Lists of applications software can be obtained from a number of sources, including RIBA Services and the CICA (see 4.2).

A few words of warning. It is extremely unwise to use a program for any sort of calculation if you are not familiar with the mathematical model on which it is based – that is, one which you don't understand, and would be unable to carry out 'manually', given time. Software, naturally, gives different results, depending on the underlying mathematical model. If you don't understand it, how will you know whether you have got a silly result, whether a mistake has been made with data input, or whether there is a bug in the program? Calculations which are used frequently and which are used as a design aid can be set up in-house, on a spreadsheet.

It is advisable to use the same range of software as your technical consultants – consult them!

Section 4

Assessing needs

So ... do you think you need a computer? Remember you are not going to buy a computer because you think you need one, but because you have a job for it to do. If at this point you know you do not need a computer but think you ought to have one to impress people, buy a secondhand machine and leave it talking to itself in a prominent corner of your office! On the other hand you may see a use for one but are totally unfamiliar with computers. 'Surely computers can do anything?', you ask. Well, perhaps they can – but at a cost.

A CAUTIONARY TALE

The members of a small practice had a pretty good idea of what they wanted a computer to do. They wanted a drafting system which would check the drawings against the Building Regulations. This sounds an entirely reasonable objective.

They received a quick brush-off from several salesmen on the lines of 'Sorry, squire – not possible. You don't know what you're talking about'. Eventually they sought help from an independent computer group who explained what such a system would have to do. It would have to:

- be able to create drawings and recognise configurations of lines as building components (a modelling system will do this);
- store the Building Regulations and all the associated documentation (possible with a large interactive data base);
- have a protocol and rules for systematically checking each element (theoretically possible using an expert system);
- carry out structural and environmental calculations and access up to date information about properties of materials (this is possible);
- allow for 'what-ifs'.

There are programs which will check parts of the Building Regulations, but by the time someone has developed a system that will 'do the lot' for any configuration and type of building, the Regulations will be amended or the data will be out of date. In any case the practice would not have been able to afford such a system had it existed.

The attitude of the salesmen was not particularly helpful, alienated the practice and made them less willing to make requests or ask questions that might seem stupid. It was eventually established that they needed, in terms of what was then available, a drafting system on which they could produce standard house types and details which were known to comply with the current Building Regulations, and a wordprocessing package that could handle standard specifications.

AND THE MORAL IS ...   It is difficult, if you know very little about computers, to know what they can do and even more difficult to know what is available; however, it is better to know what you want and ask for it, than to be talked into buying expensive hardware and software which does not fit your immediate, let alone future, needs. Time spent carefully researching and evaluating your needs is not wasted.

4.1 Evaluating practice procedures

The first step is to analyse how your practice runs. This is not as easy as it sounds because many procedures will have developed over the years which have become so integrated into the working of a practice that no one recognises them. The evaluation process may take some time and should be somebody's full-time task. It can be a sensitive operation as people will be unwilling to admit that the status quo includes bad practice or inefficient procedures. For a large practice the process is complicated as well as sensitive, and it is worth considering the appointment of a management consultant.

Quality assurance
Practices considering quality assurance have to subject themselves to stringent self-analysis and accept the possibility that administrative and technical procedures may need completely overhauling and restructuring. A manual or manuals relating to office procedures and any quality system adopted will have to be compiled. If computers are not used at present or if a change of equipment or upgrade of software is being considered, the possible computer applications should be considered in conjunction with the required office reorganisation. The checklists that follow are not comprehensive; they are intended to form a framework for investigating practice procedures. Readers will notice their similarity to the kind of analysis recommended in the context of quality assurance.

Checklist: General office management

Q. How many people are employed? Full time, part-time or contract?

Q. Are there in-house specialists? QS, structural engineer?

Q. Does everyone appear to be fully employed?

Q. Would it be acceptable to make staff redundant? Or possible to take on more staff?

Q. Is the practice making a profit, breaking even, running on overdraft, or at a loss?

Q. How far into the future does the workload appear to be assured? Could a new project be undertaken immediately?

Q. How are projects run? Who does the design, liaises with clients, consultants, site personnel? Who does the production drawings? Who looks after contractual matters?

Q. How are records kept of decisions made during a project? Does any one person have an overview?

Q. Who orders office equipment and stationery? Who takes prints, makes tea, knows where everything is?

Q. Who deals with trade reps?

Q. What equipment exists in the office and what condition is it in?

Checklist: Job running and costing

Q. Is there a standard procedure when a new job comes in?

Q. Does the practice make fee bids? On what basis?

Q. How is it decided whether a job can be undertaken? How is it decided who will run it? How is it decided whether it can make a profit?

Q. Do employees fill in timesheets? Is individual time costed against specific jobs? At what rates is staff time costed out?

Q. Is the RIBA *Architect's Job Book* (or a home-grown book of procedures) used? Is the NBS or another standard specification used?

Q. What day-to-day records are kept?

Q. How many files are kept for each job and who has access to them?

When you have checked through an exhaustive list and discussed the findings with senior staff you should be in a position to determine any areas which require further investigation, or procedures which need to be tightened up, formalised or changed. The process may unearth some salutary facts.

The questions included in the checklists are fairly random but illustrate the range of items that should be considered.

Checklist: Accounting

Q. Who keeps the books?

Q. At what intervals are accounts updated?

Q. How many ledgers are kept?

Q. What accounting system procedure is used (eg double entry)?

Q. Are the accounts linked with a formal job costing system, a PAYE system, a forecasting system?

Q. What happens to petty cash, equipment, and stationery receipts?

Q. How is VAT handled?

Q. What happens about recoverable expenses?

Q. Who administers fee accounts?

Q. Are timesheets integrated into an accounting system?

Q. Does anyone know the current financial position? If not, how long will it take them to find out?

Checklist: Secretarial tasks and administration

Q. How much time do administrative staff spend in general office activities? Typing? Filing? Answering the telephone?

Q. Is there a receptionist and/or a telephonist?

Q. Are letters written in longhand for a copy typist? Dictated for a shorthand typist or to a cassette for an audio typist? Are there numerous procedures according to individual preferences?

Q. Could all the typing be done by one person? Would this be a full-time occupation? Is this desirable? What is the optimum arrangement using existing personnel? Or hiring new personnel?

Q. Are standard letters, invoices, accounts, memoranda and instructions used?

Q. How many copies are kept of outgoing correspondence? How are copies made and by whom? How frequently are they filed?

Q. How are other records such as architects' instructions, memos, notes and telephone messages duplicated and filed?

Q. What kind of typewriters are used and when are they due for replacement?

Q. Is there a fax machine? How often and by whom is it used and how are records filed?

Q. Is there a photocopier? Can it reduce, enlarge and/or reproduce colour?

Q. Who is responsible for the maintenance of office machinery? What contracts exist and which member of staff deals with them?

Q. What is the condition of all this equipment and when is it due for replacement?

Accounting

Bookkeeping is time-consuming and exacting. Who does it clearly depends on the size of practice. Too often it is considered a chore to be done retrospectively rather than used as a creative method of controlling work and cash flow.

It is a good idea at this stage to discuss existing procedures with the practice's accountant (who will no doubt be advising you about finance if and when you decide to buy a computer). It is important to know exactly how your accounting is done and to what extent you might change it before attempting to find software that might be useful in this area. A well-organised and efficient accounting system is one of your most important assets.

Secretarial tasks and administration

Secretaries and administrators are often taken for granted but it may be that the secretaries are the only people who know what goes on in the office as a whole, because they handle the correspondence and many of the telephone calls. The absence of a secretary can often cause chaos.

All the administrative and secretarial procedures should be examined, including documentation, filing, record keeping and communications and any acceptable improvements considered.

Libraries

Most offices have a library 'system' which may mean anything from a load of catalogues residing in cardboard boxes, through a CI/SfB system to a leased system which is periodically updated. Some of the latter are available on microfiche.

A library does not only contain up to date product, legal and technical information, but also records of past jobs. How each type of information is stored, accessed and updated (if necessary) should be examined and evaluated.

Here again who does what, when and how must be determined and areas of possible improvement identified.

Drawing procedures

Drawing practice varies greatly between offices depending on the type of work, the expectations of the clients and the standards acceptable to the partners. In most procedures there is wastage and duplication of information which may or may not be necessary. It may be that design drawings also serve as contract and production drawings, especially on small jobs. On the other hand there may be extensive design drawings

---

Checklist: Library information

Q. Are case studies and job records used as feedback information?
Q. What happens to records of completed jobs and the associated drawings?
Q. How long does it take to retrieve information?
Q. What happens to trade literature? How is it filed and how long is it kept?
Q. Is technical and trade information regularly updated? By whom?
Q. Is there a microfiche?

Checklist: Drawing procedures

Q. Is a standard set of drawings used for every job? What is it?
Q. Are standard details used, for what and when?
Q. Are standard plans, generic forms or layouts used? For what and when?
Q. Is it usual to produce perspective design drawings for clients? Is this done by individual draughtsmen or by an in-house specialist? Or is such work contracted out to an expert? Why?
Q. Is the conceptual design done by one person and then 'farmed out' to others to produce design and production drawings?
Q. How are amendments made? Is a record of amendments kept other than on the drawing?
Q. How is consistency between drawings checked and ensured? Who does this and how often?
Q. How long does it take to produce an average drawing?
Q. What media are used and for what (ink, pencil, paper, tracing paper, tracing film, colour etc)?
Q. What size and scale are drawings? Why?
Q. Does the practice have a dyeline machine? When is it due for renewal? Is there a photocopier big enough to reproduce drawings?
Q. How is production information issued to site? How are amendments resulting from instructions dealt with?

---

and a set of production drawings which are produced in an entirely different format. How drawings are produced is often determined by the means of reproduction available. (Gone are the days of the tracer.)

The size of drawings is also important. This is determined by the amount of detail that can be drawn clearly to a particular scale. There is a growing tendency to use smaller drawings because A0 and A1 paper is difficult to handle, particularly on site. The media used affect the speed of drawing, and whilst there is usually a 'house style', this is not always appropriate to get maximum productivity out of all employees.

It is important to have all this information before even contemplating the use of a computer for drawing purposes.

Marketing and advertising

Nowadays the image of a firm derives largely from its marketing skills and the quality of the promotional material it produces. Existing publicity procedures, the quality of brochures, letterheads and the house-style generally must be evaluated, and suggestions made for improvement. This is explored in another title in this series.

Technical support

There are a number of specialist activities that may be carried out either by an in-house specialist, as a check on the work of consultants, or as guides to design. These include structural and environmental calculations and land surveys. It is obvious that because of the mathematical nature of such work computer programs will be available to carry it out. Whether computer techniques should be adopted will depend on the answers to the questions below.

Checklist: Technical support

Q. How much work of a specialist nature is carried out?
Q. Are the specialists prepared to work to the same mathematical model or protocol as the available software?
Q. Is the practice prepared to accept liability for results produced?

In the case of surveying, it should also be asked whether a substantial investment in the necessary equipment is possible. Output from surveying equipment will have to be fed into the existing (or proposed) drafting system.

Defining needs

All the tasks reviewed above could be done by a computer but may be quite adequately done by existing methods. Investigating the computer market will consume time and money. As has been said, large or busy practices will have to decide whether it will be more cost-effective to pay a consultant to do this analysis for them.

Now that an overall picture is beginning to emerge, you can begin to define your needs more accurately. Start by deciding what tasks are being carried out that are not the best use of someone's time. For instance, if the senior partner in a small practice has to 'waste time' drawing details or is getting snowed under by routine administrative chores, some reorganisation is clearly needed. This may require some reallocation of tasks amongst existing staff, not always an easy thing to do. It should not be based on 'who should do what', but on 'who is capable of doing what?'

If there is an unforeseen increase in workload, reallocation may be a necessity, plus the appointment of additional staff. The analysis of existing practice will help you determine the ramifications of such a contingency. In any case, you will have to judge whether the increase in fee income will cover the cost of additional staff.

If designers, technicians or draughtsmen are squandering design time on lengthy administrative tasks, a more cost-effective solution must be found.

You should examine and evaluate all practice procedures and decide what changes, if any, will result in increased efficiency. Similarly, all existing office equipment should be reviewed; perhaps in the short term a new electronic typewriter or a photocopier or a fax machine might solve any immediate difficulties.

The people exposed to this kind of study are unlikely to admit that their methods of working are inefficient, and the investigator may need to use a great deal of tact and diplomacy – not always easy.

Write up your investigations in report form and discuss it fully with the staff involved. Anyone who is wary of computers or the idea of a new system should be encouraged to see all the potential advantages. If anyone in the office is under-employed, it may be difficult to justify the use of a computer, at least until office procedures are made more efficient and staff are fully and satisfactorily deployed.

After investigation and discussion several alternative courses of action will emerge:

- do nothing
- change existing procedures
- reallocate staff responsibilities
- lose or acquire staff
- obtain additional office equipment (colour photocopier, fax machine etc)
- consider using a computer bureau for some tasks
- identify a task or tasks which could be usefully done by a computer (with help from a friendly human being)

The next step is to produce a specification for the jobs which might be carried out by the computer, the current and estimated size of these jobs in terms of volume of input, and the timescale within which each job has to be carried out (daily, weekly, monthly).

The specification need not be long, but it must be explicit and comprehensive, defining the functions expected of the computer, the total budget available for software, hardware, maintenance and training, and the timescale for installation.

What next?

Whatever the outcome of your investigations, do not pop into a high street shop and buy a computer – it will be a mistake. There is a lot more work to do before falling prey to the winning ways of salesmen! Something that you *should* do at this point is decide the amount of capital that can be made available for a computer installation. Decide on a maximum allocation and stick to it.

It will take time to determine which is the best system to adopt, time to install the equipment and time to train the personnel. Decide who will be involved in the process and how much time and money the practice can afford.

It may be reassuring to talk informally to other computer users at this stage. It is generally difficult to obtain completely independent advice, particularly free advice. The Yorkshire saying 'You don't get owt for nowt' is usually true – unfortunately in computing, you sometimes don't get owt for owt either!

Ideally, the best advice can be obtained from a practice that has had (for about a year) a system similar to the one you think you need, is about the same size, is not in direct competition and has learnt from its mistakes. As architectural practice becomes more competitive, this sort of advice may not be quite as forthcoming as in the pioneering days. But don't worry: there are people out there who can help you.

4.2 Sources of advice and consultancy

RIBA Information Technology Groups

The best bet is an independent user group. For architects in Yorkshire and Scotland (at present) there are RIBA and RIAS information technology groups who provide free advice and help and are able to give information about other computer users in the area. RIBA regional secretaries may also be able to provide some contacts.

Schools of Architecture

All schools of architecture use computers and some run short courses. The 'computer person' in each school usually has three characteristics: they are friendly, they are used to teaching people who know very little about the subject, and they are overworked. If you can catch one of these paragons of virtue [*she said modestly. Ed.*] they will be prepared to advise you about approaching the subject, but they *won't* be prepared to recommend systems. They will arrange a visit to the school (but not when they are busy) and give some tuition, for a fee. Schools, like practices, have had to become more commercially-minded, and are obliged to market the services or systems which they have developed. As a result, their advice may not necessarily be independent and, other than the odd telephone conversation, should not be assumed to be free.

User groups

There are user groups for various types of machines and for most major software packages. The groups exist for self-help and are usually prepared to assist potential users. Details of these groups can be obtained from suppliers of hardware and software and from the Construction Industry Computer Association (CICA).

Consultancy organisations

RIBA Services produce a software selector which is intended for use by architectural and related practice.

   CICA is an independent body which has information about consultants, users, hardware and software. Its consultants will give initial advice by telephone, but require payment for further services. Annual membership of CICA varies according to the size of organisation. Members receive regular bulletins and are given preferential rates for publications and consultancy. The National Computer Centre, based in Manchester, is another independent body which provides consultancy and a wide range of publications.

Exhibitions

There are numerous exhibitions of hardware and software. A visit to one of these will give you an indication of what is available, but unless you know exactly what you are looking for, take any advice offered with a pinch of salt. Everyone will be selling the 'best and most up to date' products that are 'exactly what you need'. The people who man (or woman) the stands are rarely experts: they are more often sales people who have learnt all the words but may not know what they *mean*. This may sound uncharitable, but selling has never been a charitable occupation!

Magazines

Computer magazines tend to concentrate on specific machines or aim at specialist users. Some of them are intelligible only to computer *cognoscenti*. Most of them assume that the reader understands the words, and few basic explanations are given. The best magazines are an invaluable source of information, but are not a great deal of help to the novice. The best thing the novice can do is go and talk to as many people as time and circumstances allow.

Consultants

Employing a consultant is usually not appropriate if you have a clear idea of your needs, have discussed their feasibility with an independent person and have a limited budget. At current rates (1989) a consultant will charge about £400 per man day, and the total fee may be a substantial proportion of the budget allocated for a computer installation.

A consultancy can provide a range of services from initial advice to full responsibility for the acquisition of hardware and software, installation and training. The fee for this may be negotiated as a time charge or as a lump sum. For major investments in computing equipment a consultant is essential. A good consultant will have a comprehensive knowledge of available software and will recommend the best hardware on which to run it.

Few consultants are truly independent, often having links with software houses or suppliers, but this is only to be expected. In any case, a consultant is likely to be a lot less partial than a software house. It is important to check what links a consultant has before appointment.

The advantage of using a consultancy is that as well as saving you a great deal of time, it allows the possibility of redress if an installation fails or does not meet your stated requirements.

Choosing a consultant

A glance at the Yellow Pages or at the *Computer Users Year Book* will reveal a large number of purveyors of computer expertise. As in all walks of life, some are cowboys. It is difficult to make a choice – rather like choosing a solicitor in a town where you do not know the business community, or a contractor in an area in which you have never worked. The best course of action is to write a specification for the services required and go out to tender.

Obviously the best advertisement for a consultant is a personal recommendation from a satisfied client. If you do not know any satisfied clients, ask a few consultancies to give you a list of people for whom they have worked, and then make a few careful enquiries. Make a list of potentially suitable consultants and send exactly the same information to each of them. This should consist of a specification for the performance requirements of the system, an accurate description of the services that the consultant is expected to provide, a timescale, and a budget. In addition, ask for details of similar work that the consultancy has undertaken.

From now on everyone, including consultants, is trying to sell something, and so if replies are are slow, slack or off-hand the firm is either inefficient or too busy to cope – neither bodes well for future success. Ask each potential consultant to send in a preliminary tender by a fixed date.

A good consultancy will send someone out to a potential customer to get a better idea of their needs. This service should (but may not) be free. The initial meeting is a good opportunity to get a 'feel' about the consultancy. Find out whom you will be dealing with – it may not be the person who makes the initial visit – meet them, and find out if you have any rapport. If the chemistry isn't right, it is unlikely that a good working relationship will be established. Continue this process until you are satisfied that your needs are understood and that the appropriate service can be provided.

When you have chosen a consultant, set down in writing the terms of reference for appointment, with particular attention to timescale and financial arrangements. This protects the consultant as well as the client. Clients often change their minds, particularly when they see new systems advertised which seem better than the one they have just agreed to have installed. In the computer world, the state-of-the-art changes rapidly, and if the selection process takes a long time, the system that was thought appropriate at the outset may not be so six months later.

Section 5

Selecting a system

If a consultant is not appointed (and larger practices are strongly advised to appoint one), someone in the practice will have to undertake the task of selecting a system, and will have to carry out the same investigation of available software as would a consultant.

Remember: never buy a computer and then look for software. Most software houses recommend specific hardware and, as there is no such thing as complete compatibility of hardware, you would be well advised to take their advice.

The first step is to list any software that looks likely to meet the specification. The list can be compiled from recommendations by other users, the *RIBAS Software Selector*, the technical press and catalogues available from dealers and computer exhibitions.

5.1 Exhibitions

Exhibitions have been mentioned earlier as good sources of general information. If there is no desperate hurry to install a computer, a programme of visits to exhibitions can be useful. A list of questions should be prepared in advance and if possible a list of the exhibitors showing suitable products. When you get there, don't be afraid to ask questions. The 'silly' question is often fundamental and may pinpoint the inadequacy of a system or a gap in the salesman's knowledge.

At exhibitions everyone is on show and on their best behaviour, so take the opportunity of asking how many technical support staff a company has, and the delivery, installation and training time for a product. If the stand is busy, or if it is staffed by sales rather than technical assistants, you will be asked to fill in an enquiry slip. Pick up all the catalogues and price lists you can, and compare them.

5.2 Software houses

Having drawn up a list of possible software, ask the relevant software houses for details, particularly of the total cost of the package mounted on appropriate hardware. Compare the literature and list, say, four options. Then send the specification for your requirements to each software house, requesting information on the lines of the checklist.

Checklist: Approach to a software house

Q. Will the software perform the tasks required of it without major modification?

Q. If not, how easily and at what cost can the software be customised?

Q. What is the cost of the software?

Q. What is the cost of the software plus suitable hardware (with options)?

Q. How long will the system take to install?

Q. Is training included in the cost of the software? If not, what is the cost?

Q. What are the terms of the maintenance contract?

Ask them to provide this information by a specific date. As with consultants, if the request is not answered or met, either the software house is lax or overloaded. They may, sensibly, pass on your enquiry to a local supplier, but should inform you of this. The pre-sales service is usually faster than the post-sales service so avoid potential suppliers who are slow in responding. After carefully considering the replies, ask for a demonstration of any software that looks suitable.

5.3 Demonstrations

Demonstrations are usually held at the software houses or at the premises of a supplier. The advantage of this for the seller is that there is a good chance of everything working perfectly. Similarly it is to the advantage of the prospective buyer to have a demonstration on their home ground as they can be more resistant to sales pressure and more people can observe the system. As equipment is now quite lightweight, it is not unreasonable to request this.

Salesmen generally give set demonstrations which show the full capabilities of the system and which are invariably impressive. Some are reluctant to deviate from them, usually because they are salesmen and not software experts, and do not want to get out of their depth. If a non-standard demonstration is required it is prudent to warn the software house in advance, and prepare examples of the type and format of problem or application which the computer program will be required to undertake. This applies equally to applications as simple as wordprocessing, where the fonts, type size and versatility are important, as it does to more complex programs and packages, where there will be a large number of specific requirements. A demonstration of this nature will take several hours, but is worthwhile if there is serious commitment on both sides. Ideally someone from the practice should try to use the system under the watchful eye of the salesman.

For straightforward applications such as wordprocessing, calculations and, to some extent, drafting systems, it will be easy to see whether the system fulfils the requirements. For management and financial systems it is unlikely that the software will fit existing office procedures exactly; this means that either procedures will have to be changed or the software customised. The implications of this should be considered to prevent unnecessary complications later.

Modelling systems and sophisticated drafting systems take a long time to learn and it is not easy to assess how useful they are going to be. These systems are not cheap, and you would be well advised to employ a consultant. It is also worth sending the potential operators on a familiarisation course on one or two systems before a final decision is made. This is not cheap either.

5.4 Manuals

However sophisticated and suitable software appears at demonstrations, it may be difficult to use when you are alone with nothing to help you but a manual – and these range from good to dreadful.

The problem of deciphering manuals is not confined to the novice. Learning a system is not a mysterious rite – it is like learning the rules for a new game, like chess. Individuals find they have aptitudes for different 'games', and exactly in the same sense as you cannot expect a chess master to be expert at mah-jong, there is no reason to suppose than an expert in one system will know how to operate another.

Have a good look at the manual (or manuals) before buying a system. A good manual will give instructions about what to do from when the computer is turned on, and then have a tutorial section that enables the new user to carry out increasingly complex tasks. Instructions for commands should be clear and procedures for carrying out a series of commands explicit. A section on what to do when something goes wrong or when you make a mistake is invaluable.

5.5 Training

Find out, when you are choosing a system, what training will be given and how much it will cost. Some software houses run courses which last for several days, on their own premises. The cost of these courses may or may not be included in the price of the software.

For small installations and 'off-the-peg' software a limited amount of training should be provided by the supplier, but this should not be taken for granted. In general, do not expect training and support for commonly used low cost software – a manual is provided and that's it.

5.6 Delivery and installation

There is no point in putting pressure on suppliers for quick delivery unless the office is ready for the computer. You cannot just 'plonk' it on to a desk top and expect it to be used efficiently. Space is needed for peripherals, drawings, documents, ledgers, reference books and manuals. Extra storage, shelving and layout space will be needed. You may have to provide additional wiring or socket outlets, and to modify lighting and ventilation. Desks and chairs may need replacing.

HOW NOT TO DO IT...

Even if the installation is a single wordprocessing machine and a printer on a receptionist's desk (for maximum visibility to clients at minimum capital outlay), provision should be made for dealing with trailing cables and multiple adapters. Bodges and tangles partially hidden behind a waste paper basket are bad for the 'vis. cred.' – let alone the health and safety of users and passers-by!

There is more detailed advice about environmental requirements in 7.2, about installation in 7.3, and about health and safety in 7.4.

To buy or not to buy?

It may be nobler in the mind to stop at this stage (or employ a consultant) if there is no clear indication that the acquisition of a computer is an advantage. There is no point in having a machine that doesn't perform as well as people. During the process of office investigation and software evaluation people in the practice will have gained valuable experience, got to grips with computer jargon and will be able to watch the technical press and the computer market generally for future developments. Time that has been spent in the investigation has not been wasted.

If buying a computer still seems a good idea, ask the software houses (or the suppliers they have recommended) for an estimate. If there is no clear front-runner at this point, make certain that those asked for estimates quote for exactly the same range of services. Watch out for hidden costs, which may be in training, call-out time, maintenance, updates and hardware for expanding the system.

Even the most experienced users make mistakes, particularly when buying state-of-the-art software. New, and often excellent, programs may have been developed by a small company or an individual and then marketed by its originator or by a larger company, but in either case it is unlikely that adequate technical support can be provided until enough systems are sold. In the interim period, early buyers may have to wait for help from the one or two people who understand the system. They find themselves in possession (temporarily) of useless software, word gets about and people stop buying it.

The situation is made worse if the software is sold to another house, who may not feel inclined to provide any support. The hapless buyers are left crying in the wilderness. It's amazing how fast things disappear in the computer world! The answer is to find a system which has a reasonable number of established users in the UK – but of course every system has to have a first user ...

Section 6

Choosing software

This section outlines the features that should be examined when choosing software. There is no point in buying sophisticated software if it contains many features that will never be used. Whatever its type, there are a number of questions that should be asked, which can be summed up as *Does it do what I want it to do?*

Checklist: Any software package

Q. How easy is it to use?

Q. How long will it take to learn?

Q. Can it be upgraded or expanded? Used in conjunction with other software?

Q. What is the cost of software, and hardware (with options), training, maintenance and stationery?

Q. How many established users are there?

Q. What are the arrangements for trouble-shooting? Help lines?

Q. Is the manual intelligible? Are the procedures clear? Is there a tutorial?

Technically, you do not buy the software, but the right to use it. Never accept version 1.1 of anything – it will be full of bugs. Successful software will be updated in response to feedback from users, and you should go for the most up-to-date release. Find out whether, and if so how much, you will have to pay for subsequent updates. In some applications, particularly drafting systems, software can be leased, in which case new versions should be provided free.

For the purposes of this section, software can be divided into two categories: general purpose packages and specialised applications packages which are designed for use by architects and other people in the building industry.

There are numerous packages suitable for a wide range of uses; they are not specific to one discipline, and can be bought 'off-the-peg'. The following general purpose software is described in terms of operation, terminology and desirable attributes:

Wordprocessing (6.1);
Desktop publishing (6.2);
Spreadsheets (6.3);
File management systems and databases (6.4);
Graphics and paint (6.5);
Communications (6.6).

Integrated applications software is available which includes at least a wordprocessor, spreadsheet and database, and often business graphics and communications facilities. As software is developing at a pace and each new release of each type of program contains more 'bells and whistles', it is not appropriate to describe the state-of-the-art, but rather to give a general idea of what can be expected of each type of 'tool'. Specialised software has been developed for architectural applications and this too is reviewed. It is essential to know your requirements before investigating these. The applications are:

Drafting, visualisation and modelling (6.7);
Structural, environmental and other calculations (6.8);
Office management systems (6.9);
Project management (6.10).

6.1 Wordprocessing

There are about 200 wordprocessing packages currently on the market, of which about five are market leaders. It is often tempting to buy something which you have heard of rather than spend more time looking carefully to see if the software fulfils your current and future needs. Decide at the outset what type of work the wordprocessor is expected to do. All wordprocessors will readily produce a one-page letter, and the quality of the output will depend on the software/ printer combination. The choice becomes more difficult when long and complicated documents are to be produced or the wordprocessor is required to interact with output from other programs.

If only letters are to be produced, it is often easier to use a good quality electric typewriter with a limited memory, particularly if carbon copies are required. If the system is to be used for wordprocessing only, a dedicated wordprocessor might be appropriate; a large range of these is available. At the cheap end of the market, these are often supplied as complete systems with the printer included in the price. A possible disadvantage is that the disks may be in a non-standard size or obscure format, which makes transfer to other systems difficult.

The more expensive dedicated machines are adequate provided that it is acceptable that the machine can not be used for other applications and that transfer of data from other software may be difficult.

Even the simplest wordprocessing package should have the following capabilities as a minimum:

- the creation and storage of text
- editing – correction and modification of text
- formatting – arrangement and layout of text
- printing – the production of hard copy

Text input

Wordprocessors handle text as *documents*. A document is a file containing a specific piece of text that can be as long as a report or as short as a letter. Documents are divided into pages. A page format, in terms of margins, numbers of lines, line spacing, tab settings and justification is set by the operator for each document (or page), and the software will automatically divide text into pages, without the typing having to halt.

Text can be handled as *blocks*. Blocks are pieces of text with the same format which can vary in length from a single line to several pages. Blocks (and pages) are divided into *paragraphs* (strings of characters input between two strikes of the return/enter key). Paragraphs are composed of *sentences* (text between two full stops), sentences of *lines*, lines of *words* (characters between spaces) and words of *characters*.

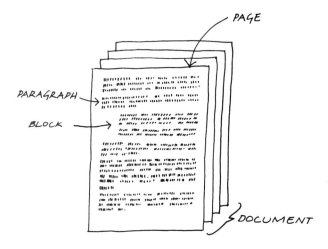

Editing

The major advantage of wordprocessors over typewriters is their editing facilities. When text is entered into a wordprocessor it exists in electronic form. If alterations are needed, any portion of text which can be recognised by the software (character, word, line, paragraph, block, page) can be amended, inserted or deleted. Methods of deleting and inserting vary between packages. Simple packages may require the delete function to be repeated until the unwanted text disappears character by character, whereas others may allow for the complete deletion of lines, sentences or paragraphs.

If parts of a document are in the wrong order, most wordprocessors allow for 'cut and paste' operations which allow elements of text to be identified and moved to a new position. The copy function, if available, allows elements of text to be copied and the copy to be 'pasted' into a new position. This is useful for repeated paragraphs.

Formatting

Page characteristics, such as number of lines and spacing are usually established when the margins and tabs are set. Margins are determined by setting the left hand margin, and then, depending on the package, the right hand margin can either be ragged or justified. If justified, the words will be spaced out to fill the line or proportionally spaced so that individual character widths are adjusted to achieve the same effect.

A word processor does not need a 'carriage return' when the end of a line is reached: a feature called 'word-wrapping' will start a new line and adjust the preceding line so that it contains only complete words, or hyphenates the last word. Some sophisticated systems allow for multiple columns.

Some packages offer a page-formatting function, which can be carried out before printing, to allow text to be paged differently. Facilities for page numbering and page headers and footers vary according to the package selected.

Ease of use

Touch-typists are used to QWERTY keyboards, and to achieve maximum typing speed and accuracy on the wordprocessor, should not have to break off to use two hands to operate a combination of keys for a control function. Problems can arise when changing tab settings and inserting paragraphs or blocks of different widths. On the other hand it can be argued that it is useful to break the flow of input before the operator proceeds with a change in text format.

There is no such thing as a standard keyboard; the position of function keys, *control, alt, delete,* and 'shift' keys and the number pad vary, even in supposedly similar machines. It is unwise to have more than one type of keyboard, or unnecessary and time-wasting mistakes may be made.

Printing

The most fundamental consideration in choosing a wordprocessor is the quality of the output. The versatility of the system largely depends on the capabilities of the printer. Wordprocessing software normally contains a printer-driver. Check to see what kind of printers the software will support, otherwise you may have to buy an extra card to support the printer of your choice.

How the software works with the screen and the printer is important. What You See on the screen should be What You Get on the printer (WYSIWYG – pronounced 'wizziwig') – or as near as maybe. The printer may have facilities that the wordprocessor cannot operate or vice versa. Requirements must be clearly specified for:

● the number and type of fonts
● single/double underlining
● bold face
● subscripts and superscripts
● pitch variation
● special symbols

Facilities

Wordprocessing packages can provide a number of useful facilities. Some of these require a large amount of memory in order to operate efficiently, and it is quicker and easier to use them if they are available on a hard disk.

SPELLING CHECK

The package contains a 'dictionary' against which words can either be checked individually, or globally, and suspect words can be identified and then corrected. Warning! Some spelling checks are American and have significantly different views about correct 'English' spelling.

Some wordprocessors provide a 'thesaurus'. This occupies a lot of memory, and is of limited benefit to the majority of users.

GLOBAL SEARCH AND REPLACE

A search can be carried out for a particular word or text string. These can be identified and replaced, individually or globally.

WORD COUNT

Words can be counted by page, by block or by document.

MAIL MERGE

Information from external files can be added to the document; for instance, names and addresses from a database can be added to standard letters.

BOILERPLATING

This allows documents to be created by using elements of text that are stored in external files. These elements can be collected and then edited.

INTEGRATION WITH OTHER SOFTWARE

Each wordprocessor has has its own format for storing data and including control commands. It may be necessary to import text from, or export to other packages. This is done by converting the data to ASCII format, which removes the control commands. This facility is essential for users who need to transfer information by disk.

Checklist: Wordprocessor

1 Hardware compatibility
If you already have a computer:
- check that the software will run on it and that there is adequate memory
- check that there is a port for the printer and that the computer, software and printer are compatible.
If you are starting from scratch:
- check the options for hardware with the dealer and make sure that you see everything up and running before you make a final decision to buy
- check that what you see on the screen is what you get on the printer – or as near as maybe
- check that the printer has sufficient capability to make full use of the wordprocessing software.

CHECKLIST: WORDPROCESSOR

2 Typing speed
Q. Is the keyboard well laid out and 'comfortable'? Are the function keys easy to reach?
Q. Are two hands needed for control commands?
Q. Is there word-wrapping? (This is essential.)
Q. Is it possible for the typist to get ahead of the screen display? (Not a good thing.)

3 Cursor movement
Q. How easy is it to move the cursor around the document?
Q. Can it be moved by a single key stroke to the beginning or end of a line?
Q. Can it be moved automatically from paragraph to paragraph, page to page, or to a specific page?

4 Margins, tabs, line-spacing
Q. How far can the right hand margin be moved?
Q. Can the right hand margin be justified? How is the line spaced to allow for this?
Q. Is there hyphenation?
Q. How many tabs can be set? Can these be handled by the printer?
Q. Are there options for single, double and triple spacing?
Q. Can the text be centred?
Q. Can a page be set up as columns?
Q. Can all the above be changed in the middle of a document or retrospectively?

5 Text editing
Q. Are there automatic facilities for editing by character, word, line, sentence, paragraph, block or page?
Q. Can the pages be reformatted automatically after editing?

6 Type styles and fonts
Q. Do the wordprocessor and printer both provide all the characters and symbols that you want to use?
Q. What about bold or italic characters, underlining, subscripts and superscripts?
Q. Are there as many fonts as you need?

7 Save functions
Q. Is the text saved automatically? Are there back-up files?

8 Facilities
Q. Is there a spelling check? Word count? Mail merge? Boilerplating? Integration with other software?

6.2 Desktop publishing

Desktop publishing (DTP) recreates the features of a publishing house and uses the same jargon, so there is a whole new vocabulary to learn. DTP systems simulate page paste up, where blocks of text can be interspersed with illustrations. Type faces, size of print, headlines, titles, headings and sub-headings can all be defined as required.

It is not likely, at present, that a first-time computer user would buy a DTP system without some experience on a wordprocessor; a good wordprocessing package with a suitable quality printer is adequate for most applications.

What you look for in a DTP system depends entirely on what you need to produce. There is an increasing number of low-cost systems available for a wide range of hardware. These are suitable for a limited range of applications but, provided they are used with a suitable printer, may be adequate, particularly for broadsheets and newsletters. A sophisticated and consequently expensive DTP system can be justified if you need to produce a large quantity of:

- illustrated reports
- brochures
- promotional material
- annotated diagrams associated with text
- illustrated academic papers

and if high quality output in a range of formats is essential. The output from a laser printer (300 dots per inch), is acceptable for reports and other office documentation. This is not as good as typesetting quality (1,200 dots per inch) and if this is what you require you can use the laser printer output up to page proof stage only. However, some DTP software is compatible with phototypesetting equipment and this should be taken into consideration at the outset. The publishing features provided by a DTP system should include:

- typesetting
- page and document layout
- inclusion of artwork and photographs
- paste up
- printing

A DTP system should be compatible with, or contain, a wordprocessor and a graphics package. In addition there should be a graphics library and a page layout program.

It is usual to input lengthy text from a wordprocessor because text creation in a DTP system is tedious, whilst input text can be moved as blocks. This means that either the DTP must be capable of reading files created by a particular wordprocessor, or that files from the wordprocessor have to be converted into ASCII format for transfer. Similarly DTP systems will accept output from some graphics and drafting programmes, whilst others have to be converted to a suitable format, such as DXF. There is no such thing as a one hundred percent accurate translation, so you must carefully consider your present and likely future input requirements.

DTP software is available for most computers and the final product depends on the printer. For business applications at present, anything other than a laser printer is inappropriate; in addition, the level of sophistication of software needed to make a DTP system significantly better than a wordprocessor demands a hard disk, adequate memory and a fast processor. If input is to be accepted from a scanner or the system operates in a windows environment, you will need a very fast processor, more memory, and a high capacity disk.

Compatibility between each item of hardware and software involved in a DTP system is crucial, and second best will not do. Make absolutely certain that the system can produce output of the nature and quality that you require and that you do not have to sit watching paint dry to avoid the boredom of waiting for the output from a drafting system or scanner to be manipulated by the DTP.

The advantage of a DTP system for practices who produce typeset work is that the typesetting can be eliminated, provided that the reduction in quality is accepted. There is a consequent reduction in cost, as finished pages can be produced in-house.

For any practice a DTP system can produce an improvement in the quality of its documentation, as page layouts can be tried out until an acceptable solution is reached. The system will allow for a page style to be selected or invented, and then the user can experiment with the number and layout of columns, fonts, headers and footers and the position of frames containing illustrative material. The text can be made to flow around frames or to run around shapes. If the result is not satisfactory it can easily be changed.

If you do not have a computer, consider buying a complete DTP system, with a good wordprocessor and dedicated hardware. There is no point in desktop publishing if the result is unsatisfactory. It's like producing copies of *haute couture* clothes, at home, on a superannuated manual sewing machine!

Checklist: DTP systems

1 Hardware compatibility

If you are using a wordprocessing system:

- check whether the computer can support DTP software of an appropriate quality
- check the peripherals carefully, particularly the printer. Is a scanner needed? Quality of output from scanners varies in terms of the capabilities of the scanner and the type of material to be scanned. (Scanned line work is better than scanned photographs.)

2 Ease of use

Q. Who will be using the system?

Some DTP systems are aimed at computer people, some at graphic designers. Some allow text from a wordprocessor to be input into a predetermined style of page layout and illustrations to be inserted as desired in frames; others rely on experience in page layout and cut and paste operations, where both text and illustrations are handled as blocks.

Q. Is the manual is easy to understand?

Some are totally incomprehensible to users who are unfamiliar with computer and typesetting jargon.

Q. Can the whole page be viewed clearly at one time? (Not possible on all systems.) Although some systems claim WYSIWYG (see 6.1), it may not be possible to read, or even decipher text that has been *greeked*, in order to produce a view of the whole page that will fit on a screen. Greeking saves time because the text is produced as blocks of scribble rather than distinct characters, but can be infuriating when careful cutting and pasting of text is required.

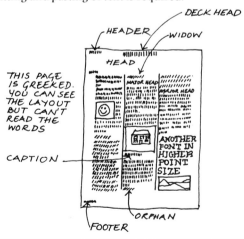

CHECKLIST: DTP SYSTEMS

Q. Are you clear about what the system will be required to handle? Obviously systems have differing strengths and weaknesses and different ways of handling information. Some are suitable for single-page layouts (suitable for short intricate documents, advertising copy and data sheets), and some for much longer documents which have been input from text files.

3 Typesetting

Q. Does the system accept input from the wordprocessing package that you use?

Q. Does the system provide enough fonts in a sufficient range of point sizes? What is the cost of extra fonts?

Q. How does the system handle right hand justification? Is there kerning? (Where the space between individual letters is increased or reduced to improve the appearance of text.)

Q. Is there proportional spacing?

Q. Is there hyphenation? Are words divided at sensible points?

Q. Is there provision for italic and bold text, and for changes between upper and lower case for individual words?

Q. Is there provision for mathematical and special symbols, subscripts, superscripts and underlining?

Q. Are bullets available ('solid' spots often used to emphasise indented text)?

4 Layout

Q. Can the page be set up as portrait and as landscape?

Q. How easy is it to set up a page, define horizontal and vertical rulers?

Q. How easy is it to create new tags and a hierarchy of titles, headings and sub-headings?

Q. How many columns can be set up?

Q. How are widows and orphans handled ('left-over' lines of text, or words – see Glossary)?

Q. How easy is it to create and then move frames? Is it possible to create captions? To draw a box around a frame?

4 Inclusion of artwork and photographs

Q. Does the system contain a graphics package? Does it do everything that you want it to do?

Q. Can input from other systems be accepted? Is there compatibility with drafting systems, paint systems, and the format for scanned images?

Q. How easy is it and how long does it take to frame-fit or crop drawings or images?

Q. Is there a library of graphics in the system?

> **CHECKLIST: DTP SYSTEMS**
>
> **5 Paste up**
> Q. How easy is it to move blocks of text and pictures? Can text be made to flow around pictures?
> Q. How long does it take to set up a page?
>
> **6 Printing**
> Q. Can the printer produce the page characteristics created on the DTP?
> Q. Is there a page description language which allows direct transfer to a typesetting machine?
> Q. Most laser printers are A4; will this cause problems? Will you need an enlarging photocopier?

6.3 Spreadsheets

A spreadsheet is an electronic work-sheet which enables the user to carry out calculations using a large amount of variable data and to forecast the effects of 'what-ifs'.

It can be imagined as a sheet of paper ruled out into rows and columns to form a matrix composed of a lot of little boxes. Each of these boxes is known as a *cell*. The columns are identified by letters (A–Z, AA–AZ, BA–BZ etc) and the rows by numerals; therefore each cell can be identified uniquely – A1, AG45, BK56 and so on. One of three types of data can be entered into a particular cell: text, numbers, or formulae.

The text can be a label, instruction, commentary or comment; numbers are numbers, and formulae may be mathematical or show the relationship between the data contained in cells.

The use of spreadsheets began with accountancy-related applications and has developed into general use because the arithmetic can be carried out easily, and spreadsheets are relatively simple to customise for specific numeric tasks. They are also useful for keeping records where numeric data may change frequently.

They range from the simple 'workpad' to sophisticated systems which allow for interactive calculations between thousands of cells and the inclusion of, or interaction with, wordprocessing, graphics and/or database software; these form the basis for many integrated office management systems.

The figures opposite are simplified examples of how a spreadsheet

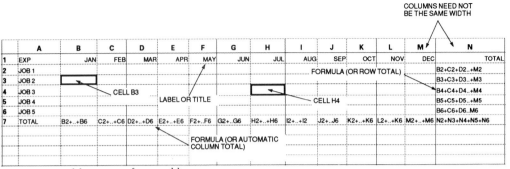

Spreadsheet set up for monthly expenses

A	B	C	D	E	F	G	H	I	J	K	L	M	N
EXP	JAN	FEB	MAR	APR	MAY	JUN	JUL	AUG	SEP	OCT	NOV	DEC	TOTAL
JOB 1		300	300			1000			200	200	200		2200
JOB 2	700				100	100	100						1000
JOB 3	2000	200	200	200	200	200	200	200	200	200	400		4200
JOB 4	500	300	100						100		100		1100
JOB 5								1000			1000		2000
TOTAL	3200	800	600	200	300	1300	300	1200	500	400	1700		10500

Spreadsheet with data input

could be used to monitor expenses. Column A contains the titles of current jobs, say JOB1 to JOB5, in cells A2, A3, A4, A5 and A6. Row 1, from B1 to M1, contains titles; in this case months of the year. Cells B2 to M2 contain projected monthly expenses for JOB1; cells B3 to M3 for JOB2, and so on to B6 to M6. N2 to N6 contain a formula which gives the total annual expenses for each job, B7 to M7 one which gives the monthly expenses for all jobs. N7 contains the annual total.

It takes time and experience to determine the best way to set out a spreadsheet. Whether this operation is carried out by the user or by a paid 'expert' it is essential that a clear description of the problem, the way it is to be solved and the amount of variable data is provided in advance. The more complex the problem the more likely it is that special facilities will be required in the spreadsheet.

When it has been established that a spreadsheet is large enough and fast enough to cope with the type of application that you intend, the most important consideration in choosing an appropriate package is whether it is easy to use, particularly if you intend to set it up yourself and use it as general office tool.

Look at the documentation and make sure that it is clear, unambiguous and that it contains a tutorial. After the initial learning period, it wastes time to have to refer frequently to the manual. There may be a number of functions that are not used very often or the user may make a careless mistake; in cases like this it is useful to have an on-screen help function.

It should be easy to set up labels, titles and headings, for columns and rows; to set the width for columns and to define the display format for entries in cells. Numeric data may be integer, fixed-point, floating-point (scientific notation) or in a special format such as time, date or currency. Text, formulae and numerals may be left or right hand justified or centred.

The package may be menu- or command-driven and in either case it should be easy to move the cursor from cell to cell, or to go to a specific location. It is essential to be able to view the contents of a particular cell even if it is not totally visible on the complete spreadsheet.

When using a large sheet it will not be possible to view the whole of it on the screen. Some packages provide windows, so that the screen can be split horizontally, vertically or both, and widely separated portions of the sheet viewed simultaneously. Where windows are not provided it should be possible to 'fix' the labels on the screen while the rest of the spreadsheet is scrolled.

Having checked for usability, make sure that the package has sufficient mathematical and logical functions to carry out the range of calculations that you will require. Also check that the system allows previously entered data to be edited. It may be possible to move whole columns or rows or sections of the spreadsheet. Methods of deletion and insertion vary as does the ability to copy the contents of one row or column into another. Some systems allow for the contents of rows or columns to be sorted into ascending or descending order.

A procedural language may be included for the creation of macros, shortcut commands which represent a series of instructions, which can be written to carry out commonly used functions. These help to improve speed and efficiency.

Graphics software may be included in the system, which will allow graphs, pie-charts and histograms to be produced, sometimes in colour. Other software may be linked or included as add-ins. A spreadsheet combined with graphics, database and wordprocessor is a powerful general purpose tool.

Printout needs careful consideration. Spreadsheets tend to be wider than they are long. Printing can be handled using a wide carriage printer, sections can be produced and then stuck together, or the system must contain a utility to handle sideways printing.

Checklist: Spreadsheets

1 Compatibility

If you already have a computer, check that there is sufficient memory to use the spreadsheet and that there is enough disk space to mount it.

A new user is unlikely to buy a computer solely to support a spreadsheet, so space requirements and compatibility must be considered in conjunction with other applications.

2 Size and speed

Q. Is the spreadsheet large enough for the proposed application?

Q. How long do typical calculations take? How long does a global recalculation take?

Q. Is there adequate file storage? How fast can files be retrieved?

3 Ease of use

Q. Is the system menu- or command-driven?

Q. How easy is it to set up a new spreadsheet?

Q. How easy is it to set up labels?

Q. How easy is it to move the cursor between cells or to a specific cell?

Q. Is there adequate on-screen help?

4 Format

Q. Is there provision for setting column widths?

Q. What are the maximum and minimum cell widths? Is it possible to format an individual cell, a single column or a particular section?

Q. What are the possible formats for numerals (integer, fixed-point etc)?

Q. Can the contents of cells be left or right hand justified, or centred?

5 Editing

Q. What sort of editing can be carried out?

Q. Can columns and rows be modified easily? Can they be inserted or deleted? Copied? 'Blanked'?

Q. Can whole rows or columns be moved?

Q. How easy is it to modify the contents of single cells?

6 Windows

Q. Are there windows that allow several areas of the spreadsheet to be viewed on-screen at one time? If so, how many? If not, is it possible to retain labels on screen when scrolling?

7 Functions and facilities

Q. Are there sufficient mathematical and logical functions?

Q. Can columns or rows be arranged in ascending or descending order?

Q. Is there a procedural language for creating macros?

Q. What other add-ins are available?

CHECKLIST: SPREADSHEETS

8 Data interchange
Q. Are the files created by the system compatible with other software?
Q. Can data from other software be converted automatically?

9 Printing
Q. What range of printers can produce hard copy?
Q. Can a print file be created and stored?
Q. Can all the spreadsheet be printed?

6.4 File management systems and databases

Both these storage and retrieval systems can be loosely described as electronic filing cabinets.

At two recent seminars on the subject of computer applications in the construction industry it was suggested that databases are a waste of time for architects, and that a file-handling system is usually adequate. There is some truth in this, but ...

The problem is one of definition: some file-handling systems are called databases, and the terminology varies idiosyncratically between both types of system. The user, of course, has not the slightest interest in the niceties of terminology provided the package will store and access information quickly and accurately. However the first-time buyer may be confused by the variations and find it difficult to compare like with like.

The terminology used in this section is consistent internally, but is not used universally in the same way.

A database is a large collection of information, structured to allow access in different ways for different applications. A database may contain a number of related files. A file is an organised collection of *records* (information); a record is a collection of related items of data which together can be treated as a unit. For example, police crime statistics constitute a *database*, stolen cars a *file*, and details of each theft are a *record*. And within a record there are *fields*. These are areas reserved for a particular type of information (car number, owner, time of theft, location of theft and so on). Fields may be of fixed or variable length in their number of characters (alphanumeric symbols). To allow records to be identified, they must contain a unique key field or fields.

The advantage of computer systems over manual storage systems is that they can be searched fast and systematically. How fast and how efficiently depends on how the files are organised and accessed.

File organisation

SERIAL FILES Records are stored in the order in which they are entered, rather like starting at the beginning of a notebook and keeping addresses and telephone numbers in the order in which they are given to you. This means that the file has to be searched from beginning to the end to find a particular record. This type of file organisation is inefficient and rarely used.

SEQUENTIAL FILES These are arranged in ascending or descending key order; the file is then searched sequentially until the desired key is found. The addresses and telephone numbers are now kept in alphabetical order.

INDEXED SEQUENTIAL FILES As a record is stored its address is written in an index. The file can either be searched sequentially or, if only a few records are required, records can be accessed directly by searching the index. The addresses and telephone numbers are kept in alphabetical order in an book with a number of indexed pages for each letter of the alphabet.

DIRECT FILES Direct file systems are used where information is always processed in a random fashion. A record can be accessed without the system having to go through other records first. There is a direct link between the key and its storage address. If an address book were organised like this, it would be possible to turn straight to a particular surname.

Databases have developed from file management systems and these allow the user to make an enquiry that can eliminate unwanted data and records. A database may be a single file or an integrated set of related files, the important point being that it can be accessed in different ways for different applications.

Not only is the relationship between records important but also the relationship of the fields within them. If a change is made to one item of data it will ideally only have to be made once, and all related files will also be updated. Taking the address book analogy again, it might contain information about people who were friends and also details of contractors, clients and other business associates. Provided that the fields were consistently defined, it would be possible to find the address of a friend called Lovelace, or for a different application to make a list of known contractors in Leeds and Bradford.

Structure of databases

A database can be viewed in three ways: conceptually, logically and physically.

The conceptual model is the overall view of the data that needs to be stored and how it is related. At this level you are not concerned with what kind of database to use but with the identification of all the record types that might be used within your organisation, the relationships between them and the fields within them.

The logical view concerns the way the data can be organised to form a database and the physical view of how it is stored. The conversion of the logical to the physical database is carried out by a database management system (DBMS).

There are three commonly used logical models: hierarchical, network, and relational. In the hierarchical model, records and data fields are related by a parent–child relationship. One parent can have several children, but not vice versa; the network model allows a 'child' to have a number of 'parents'.

The relational model, which is usually used on microcomputers, is entirely different as there is no predefined logical structure. The database is built from tables which define the relationships between records and fields.

Complexity v simplicity

If you are considering a filer or a database, you do not need to know the internal data and file management structure of a system, but you must have a very clear idea of the conceptual organisation of the data which you wish to store and retrieve.

Imagine that a database were to to be used to prepare a fee bid. How many files would have to be accessed and for what information?

You might begin with staff records, for details of salaries; then a work load planning file, to ascertain time available and availability of staff; and then files relating to similar jobs, accounts files, the client file and so on. The point is that there are many ways of doing the job manually, but if you are going to use a computer system there must be a set procedure and that procedure must be defined.

Setting up a database requires time, not only to organise the data but for the tedious and necessarily meticulous task of inputting it. Consider

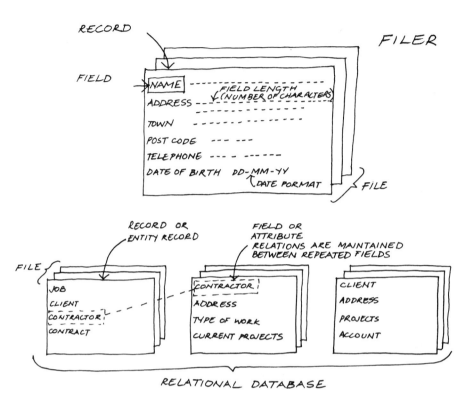

carefully the completeness and accuracy of existing manual records, how long it will take to decide what you need to do with them and how they relate, how long to set up the data on a computer system and how much time is involved in keeping it up to date. An inaccurate or incomplete database is useless. If even 5% is inaccurate it will lose its credibility and will not be used. Computers are expected to be more accurate and reliable than people and filing cabinets!

Databases are an asset, provided your organisation can cope with the time and expense involved in setting them up; small practices generally do not have the resources. Simple computer-based filers can be extremely useful and are relatively easy to use and set up. They can be used for sets of records, which are used and updated frequently, in the same way as sets of card indexes.

Office management and job costing software
Another option is to investigate the use of office management systems that are specifically designed for your type of practice. These are

usually based on a database or on the combination of a wordprocessor, database and spreadsheet. They allow for customisation, but it is not cheap. You may have to find the closest fit to your existing procedures and then change your procedures to suit. On the plus side, the data structures and relationships are predetermined and can be explained to you and set up by the vendors.

Yet another option (not for first-time users, small practices or the faint of heart) is to buy a general purpose integrated software package containing wordprocessing, spreadsheet and database and possibly business graphics, paint and communications. These can be customised, but it is impossible to customise efficiently if the customer's needs are not completely and precisely defined. These systems are complex and need to be set up and used properly. To work well they need to be maintained by dedicated people who understand the system thoroughly.

SECURITY

Security of computer systems is discussed in 7.4, but should be considered specifically in relation to stored data.

If electronically stored information is to be useful, it must allow access by more than one person. In manual systems some people have keys to particular filing cabinets, whilst others do not. Very few staff are likely to have access to all the filing cabinets, let alone the office safe. It is essential to limit access to computer data in a similar way.

Different levels of access can be protected by passwords. These give defence against casual, accidental or unauthorised access, but be warned: a talented and dedicated hacker can get into anything, given time and luck. The important point here is that a decision about who is and is not to have access must be made *before* the database or filer is set up, as this will affect *how* it is set up.

Back-up copies of data kept on hard disk should be made frequently, and always after new data is entered. Spikes in the electricity supply, power failure and accidental or malicious reformatting of the disk can result in data being lost. The floppy disks on which back-up copies are commonly made are vulnerable to damp, rough treatment, dust and magnetic fields – and they are much easier to pop into a pocket than the contents of a couple of manila files. Floppy disks should be clearly labelled, indexed and dated, and stored systematically in dustproof, locked containers. Disks stored in this way and kept in fireproof cabinets are as susceptible to fire as paper stored in the same way.

Many practices keep hard copy of everything (so much for the paperless office!). Installing computers for administrative and management purposes is not likely to save space, unless you are prepared to arrange the safe storage of back-up data.

If you are keeping data about individuals you should check your position under the *Data Protection Act* (see 7.4).

Checklist: File management systems and databases

1 Purpose
Are you absolutely clear about what you want from the system and the nature, relationship and amount of data you want to store? This is important. With other applications you can learn to use the system and then put up with or get around areas of inadequacy. It is essential that you know how you want your data to be organised otherwise it will be impossible to choose a suitable system. You may need to employ a consultant. If you are intending to user a filer, make sure that you know what you want to keep on it, and how this will need to be expanded.

2 Hardware compatibility
Check that there is enough memory to run the software. As with spreadsheets, a new user is unlikely to buy a computer solely to support a filer or database, so that memory, speed and storage requirements should be considered in conjunction with other applications.

3 Size and speed
Q. Can the software support all the files, records and fields that you need?
Q. How many files (relations) can be created and stored? How many records (entities) per file? How many fields (attributes, data items, data elements) per record? How many characters per field?
Q. How long does it take to create a record?
Q. How long does it take to access a record?

4 Operation and ease of use
Q. Is the system operated by commands or menus? Are these easy to understand?
Q. Do you have to know the structure of the system to be able to use it?
Q. Is the procedure for setting up the system made absolutely clear?
Q. Is it possible to create a form for records?
Q. Is entry of records dictated by the system?
Q. Are there enough prompts or on-screen instructions to make either of the above easy?
Q. Is there an adequate on-screen help facility?
Q. Does the system warn you when you have done something stupid? Does it tell you how to retrieve the situation?

CHECKLIST: WORDPROCESSOR

5 Data access and retrieval
Q. How is data accessed?
Q. Are records accessed sequentially? By index? By key field? By a
    combination of fields? How many?
Q. Can more than one file be searched?
Q. Are logical expressions permitted (for example, 'if x, then y')?

6 Editing
Q. Is it possible to correct data during input?
Q. How easy is it to amend a record? Can this be done accidentally?
Q. How easy is it to create a new record? To add new fields to an
    existing?
Q. How easy is it to delete a record?

7 Security
Q. Is the security provision adequate?
Q. Does the package include passwords?

8 Functions and facilities
Q. What other 'goodies' are provided?
Q. Is there a procedural language?
Q. Is it possible to create and print reports?
Q. Can mathematical or statistical operations be carried out?

9 Data interchange
Q. Can the database/filer accept input from other software? Can the
    output be accepted by other software?

6.5 Graphics and paint

These systems are easy to understand because they do exactly what
you expect them to do: they draw and colour-in! Graphics packages
range from simple business graphics of the type that is often included
in integrated management software, to sophisticated graphics and
paint systems used for specialisms such as textile design.

Until recently scientific and engineering graphic systems were
command-driven, often with obscure procedures, and took a long time
to learn. Business users have required interfaces that are much less
'technical'; this has resulted in the development of business graphics
software which is either menu-driven or uses windows and icons. The
latter is the emerging standard for all graphics applications, although

this has not been taken up for technical applications with the speed that might be expected.

Graphics for simple games and home computers can be produced using patterns of graphic or alphanumeric symbols and reproduced on a printer in the same way as text. This quality is not suitable for work where a professional standard is required.

Business graphics, at the most basic level, allows input of numeric data to produce graphs, histograms and/or pie charts. In integrated software the input can be from a spreadsheet or database. Some systems allow for three-dimensional representations (for example, showing a histogram as blocks, or removing a wedge from a pie) and/or for the use of colour.

The next level of graphics allows lines, rectangles and circles (or polygons) to be created and placed on a screen image. There may also be a library of images, symbols or patterns which can be inserted on screen. (Colour may be available in these systems and can generally be used to fill any closed polygons.) It may be possible to manipulate shapes or images by copying, mirroring, moving or extrusion, thus allowing patterns to be created. Graphic capabilities of this level are often included in desktop publishing systems, and some of the latest releases of wordprocessors have a limited capability of this type.

Stand-alone graphics systems allow drawing or sketching as well as the manipulation of predefined shapes. The user 'draws on the screen' by moving a mouse (or other input device). Drawings may be input as a series of straight lines often with *rubber-banding*. This means that the beginning of a line is marked on screen, and the 'line' is attached to the second point, which can be moved dynamically until the appropriate location is reached. On professional systems a variety of curves and closed shapes can be created. When a shape has been created (and provided it is closed) it can be filled with a pattern or tone. It should be possible to move, copy, scale or rotate parts of the drawing. There may be also be 'paint' facilities which allow texture to be applied by brush or spray, but this is of limited use in monochrome.

Paint systems allow most or all of the above, but also allow colour to be applied. This can be done in a variety of brush widths or by air spray. Paint systems are fun – the temptation to play with them is hard to resist! In crude form they are available on the type of computer used in primary schools, which has a limited number of colours and a low resolution screen. For professional use a high resolution screen is essential. Some, but not all, paint and graphics programs allow drawings from other graphics and drafting systems to be imported. If you need this facility it is essential to check whether it is available and what input format is acceptable.

To work on colour and graphics, higher screen resolution is needed than for text. The screen resolution is the number of picture elements, *pixels*, that form the display. This is typically 640 x 200 for CGA, 640 x 350 for an EGA screen and 640 x 480 for a VGA. The current set of graphic standards (CGA, EGA, and VGA) require the software to calculate and plot each pixel on the screen, so you will appreciate that a 'bit-mapped' image will take up a substantial chunk of memory.

There are additional colours available on EGA and VGA which also bump up the memory requirements. These increase from 16k for CGA resolution to to 154k for VGA. These images can be reproduced using a printer, but not on a plotter, because plotters draw lines, *vectors*.

The reproduction of screen colour as hard copy is an area of rapid development. If you are at all familiar with colour theory you will know that on a screen colours are produced by *adding* light in combinations of red, blue and green dots which if mixed equally are perceived by the human eye as white. Printers produce colour using pigment and the light seen is reflected. Pigments work by absorbing the light of some wavelengths and reflecting others; this means that if an object appears blue it is reflecting blue and absorbing all other colours. This system is known as *subtractive* and uses magenta, cyan and yellow to delete various wavelengths; the three mixed together appear black.

There are numerical ways of defining colours in both the additive and subtractive systems, but there are other aspects of colour that need to be defined: brightness and saturation. The definition of a screen colour is relatively simple; reproducing the same colour on a printer is not! However, there are available books of samples which show how screen defined colours will appear when printed in a variety of media. At the moment the best way of colour-matching what appears on the screen is done by advanced photographic techniques. This is expensive.

The colour laser printers which are now appearing on the market are as yet prohibitively expensive, but this may change. The existing affordable technologies are *film recording, dot matrix printing, pen plotting, ink jet printing* and *thermal wax transfer*.

There are two types of film recorder: *digital*, which takes digital output from the computer, and *analogue*, which takes data from the video output of a high resolution display. These recorders produce 35mm slides. Film recorders are not cheap (£3,000 to £4,500 at 1989 prices) but can be justified if slide output is required. Dot matrix printers are limited by the number of colours available and by low resolution; pen plotting by the number of pens and the restriction of the output to coloured lines.

The most common techniques for producing hard copy of reasonable quality are ink jet and thermal wax printing. The quality of both should be examined as either might be adequate for a specific purpose. Ink jet printers do not give close colour matching, and the resolution is not as good as that from a laser printer. At present, thermal transfer techniques give better resolution and colour-matching.

The gap in performance between colour screens and colour printing is closing. Keep an eye on technology, and check for developments.

Visualisation

Professional graphics systems can provide for three-dimensional representation of objects using both colour and shading. Architects would usually look for these facilities in association with a drafting or modelling system.

Checklist: Graphics and paint

1 Purpose
Decide whether you need a stand-alone graphics or paint system. Remember that limited graphics is available in some wordprocessing systems, DTP, spreadsheets and databases. If you want to draw, consider a drafting package. Have a clear idea of what you want the system to do.

2 Hardware compatibility
If you have a computer check the following:
Q. Will the software run on existing hardware?
Q. Is a higher resolution screen and graphics card needed?
Q. Is the memory adequate?
Q. What sort of printer will produce the required quality of hard copy?
   Is it compatible?

If you are starting from scratch, consider graphics and paint in relation to other applications and determine the specification for hardware accordingly.

3 Ease of use
Q. How easy is the system to use?
Q. How is it driven? By menus? By windows and icons?
Q. Is there on-screen help?

CHECKLIST: GRAPHICS AND PAINT

4 Capabilities

For business graphics:

Q. Can the system produce graphs, histograms or pie-charts from input data?

Q. Are 'extras' needed, like 3D representation or colour?

Q. Can text be added? Can it be spaced as desired?

For general purpose graphics:

Q. What shapes are provided?

Q. Is there a library of patterns or symbols?

Q. Is there a facility for 'free-hand' drawing?

Q. Is there rubber-banding on lines?

Q. Is it possible to manipulate parts of the drawing by rotation, copying, extrusion, scaling or moving?

Q. Can text be added? In what range of fonts and sizes?

Q. Is there a range of brushes or sprays for applying textures?

Q. How easy is it to overdraw or erase?

In addition, for paint systems:

Q. How many colours are available?

Q. Is it possible to produce accurately specified colours? How? What can be coloured?

Q. Can colours be changed globally? On specified portions of the screen?

Q. Is there a variety of brushes, sprays and textures?

5 Printing

Check the capabilities and price of hardware. Make sure that the quality of hard copy is of a good enough standard. Can you manage without a printer? Is photographic reproduction acceptable?

6 Data interchange

If you want to colour drawings input from graphic or drafting systems make sure that this facility is available.

6.6 Communications

Computers are able to communicate electronically. They can be physically connected by wires or cables in a Local Area Network (LAN), or by telephone, microwave or radio signals in a Wide Area Network (WAN).

Networks can be set up in several forms. A hierarchical network is one in which several computers are connected to a single computer which holds all or most of the data. This requires a multi-user operating system. Individual computers may be able to communicate with one another through the master unit. In a ring network each computer is connected to the next one to form a ring. Each computer has its own identifier and signals are passed round the ring in one direction only, each machine accepting data addressed to it. Individual computers perform their own functions and retain their own data, but this may be accessed by others in the ring. In a star network, each computer is connected to every other computer. This has the advantage of speeding up communications, but if extra computers are to be added it makes wiring complicated. Hybrid networks contain a mixture of all three systems.

If you are considering setting up a practice network you should take expert advice from the start. First-time users are advised to become familiar with the use of computers before embarking on a costly network.

Communications software (or firmware) in conjunction with a *modem*, a device which allows computer data to be transmitted on telephones, enables your computer to:

- send and receive data by telephone link to and from computers using similar devices
- search public databases on larger computers
- load and save whole programs stored on other computers
- use electronic mail
- use bulletin boards
- hack (oops!) ... but remember if you can get into other people's computers, someone can get into yours!

Fortunately, or unfortunately for hackers, communication between computers is not straightforward. In order to communicate, two machines must be using the same communications parameters. Modems (short for MOdulator/DEModulator) convert digital signals from the computer to analogue signals used in telecommunications. Signals are generally but not necessarily sent in ASCII code; this may be in 7 or 8 bits with a number of bits to show when it starts and ends, and to show whether the check sum of the bits is even or odd (parity). Often 7 bits are transmitted to describe the character, with a stop, start and parity bit, making ten bits per character, but there are many variations to this pattern. The receiving and sending modem must be set up to receive the same pattern or the result will be gook.

Checklist: Communications

1 Networks
These should not be considered by a first-time user without advice from a consultant. Get to know something about computer techniques and capabilities and the people associated with them before embarking on a major installation.

2 External communications
If you want to communicate with another branch of your organisation make sure that you have the same protocol for transmitting data. If this data is sensitive make sure that it is possible to restrict access to it. If you want to use electronic mail and/or public databases find out how much this costs either as connect time or subscription.

3 Software or firmware
Ideally it should have the following facilities:
- on-line help
- received data capable of being stored in the computer's available memory (text buffer)
- data format and parity setting
- keyboard macros to allow you to store routines for complicated protocols and procedures for logging into other computers
- auto-dial. Some modems can be programmed so that frequently accessed numbers can be dialled from a keyboard command
- auto-answer. This means that the modem can answer the telephone. It also means that unless you have security protection (levels of password), other people can access your computer.

This is a complicated area. The costs involved are not only for hardware, software, maintenance and personnel, but for subscription charges, connect-time and BT charges. The consequences of getting it wrong are costly.

Transmission speeds vary. The baud rate (bits transmitted per second) can be 75, 110, 300, 600, 1,200, 2,400, 4,800, 9,600. The speeds are determined by the communications software and the modem. Mismatches do not make for easy communication. Another difficulty arises out of the type of plug or pin that connects the computer to the modem. There is no standardisation between plugs, sockets and the nature of the signal that is transmitted down each wire. There are further complications: transmissions may be asynchronous or synchronous, half or full duplex.

Find out what or with whom you need to communicate and then

ask an expert how to do it. Not only do you want trouble-free communications, but you may need to protect your own system from unauthorised access. The latest edition of the *Hacker's Handbook* (see the Bibliography) is not only an excellent reference for those people interested in communications, but also demonstrates what 'baddies' can do if they try.

6.7 Modelling, visualisation and drafting

In an ideal world, a full model of a building could be constructed inside the computer, each part being input once only, and any plan, section, elevation or three-dimensional representation could be produced automatically. To do this, the designer would have to be capable of conceptualising and remembering a full three-dimensional model – a computer can do the remembering. Architects don't work like that!

It can be argued that in the past the tools available to the designer dictated the sort of buildings that were built. Medieval masons produced sketches for cathedrals on small areas of parchment, set buildings out on site using geometric principles and pragmatism, and set out areas of vertical stonework horizontally, on a tracing floor, before they were erected. Fine detail was the province of individual craftsmen. The buildings produced were structurally and construc-tionally repetitive – big mediaeval Lego!

Because of the slow and fastidious drawing methods available to nineteenth and early twentieth century designers, the number of drawings was limited, usually to eighth-scale arrangement drawings and to quarter- and full-size details. Reproduction of drawings was limited to manual copying and later tracings. The translation of an idea into a building relied on a limited number of unambiguous drawings and a high degree of craftsmanship on the part of builders.

Tracing paper and the advent of dye-line printing speeded things up. More drawings in less time, more flexibility – more scope for lack of co-ordination, more likelihood of mistakes.

Did the buildings produced by the lesser adherents to the Modern Movement result from the introduction of parallel motion and designers who were so besotted with their new 'toy' that they forgot to use their adjustable set-squares and French curves?

Should the tools available dictate what is designed? It is always a temptation, when you are in a hurry, to use only what is available. The early computer drafting and modelling systems were (and many still are) bad at handling curves, complex roof geometry and internal changes in level. Result? Early users avoided curves, complex roof geometry and internal changes in level, or at least did not use a computer to produce them.

On the other hand, surely a designer should make full use of the available tools, even if this entails a fairly drastic change in working methods, particularly if the result is a better finished product (building, not drawing)?

Modelling

There are a number of sophisticated modelling systems. These are at the high end of the market and require a fast processor and a large amount of memory, not available on what are at present commonly considered to be microcomputers. These systems allow a building model to be created and attributes assigned to the 'stuff' of which components are made. Predictive modelling can then be carried out for, say, thermal, lighting and structural performance. This sort of total building performance analysis is not normally carried out by practices. (It's all very well in a university!) Architects tend to rely on experience, rules-of-thumb and advice from specialists. The computer modeller will not necessarily save time, but could produce, at least in terms of performance, a better product and better quality control.

The use of a modeller will involve a change in working methods and the acceptance of the concept that the building is designed as a full-size, dynamic model, and not as a series of drawings. If your existing design procedures are satisfactory, but you want to produce drawings on a computer, you do not need a modelling system – yet.

Perhaps modellers at present are not quite up to what could, ideally, be expected of them, but technology is changing fast and by the time you read this book things may have improved significantly. Meanwhile a compromise might be to consider a limited modeller, which will handle perspectives or a range of performance calculations, which might meet your needs and will run on a microcomputer.

State-of-the-art modelling will not be considered in any more detail, and in any case this kind of application is not advisable for first-time users. If you already have a computer, and think you are ready for something bigger, the usual general principles apply. Does it do what you want it to do? If it doesn't, forget it for a while or look for something else. Watch the technical press, keep in touch with software developments, explore the full capabilities of any system and decide whether you would use them in practice.

Visualisation

Modellers can be used for visualisation. The client can be 'flown' around the outside of the building, land, approach on foot, be taken into his third floor office, and find himself sitting at his own desk. This is state-of-the-art, costly in time and money alike.

There is some overlap between drafting, visualisation and modelling. As software develops, drafting systems acquire visualisation features, and modellers can be linked to drafting of an acceptable standard.

In terms of architectural design it is convenient, if not particularly accurate to the purist, to say that wire-line and surface modellers are for visualisation, by which is meant a means of testing the appearance of something.

Some systems, which started their life purely as drafting tools, now have in-built programs which allow perspectives as wire-line representations to be generated, sometimes with hidden line removal. What drafting systems and wire-line modellers have in common is that input is by the definition of lines which represent edges – drafting systems in one plane, modelling systems in many. True wire-line modellers allow reality to be defined by lines representing edges or boundaries in three-dimensional space.

Further programs may allow for the addition of colour. To the layman, there is little difference between the output from these and limited surface modellers.

Visualisation ranges from wire-frame perspectives used as a base for presentation drawings, through systems that can produce coloured and shaded surfaces for, say, internal perspectives, to animation.

Drafting

Drafting systems draw; they do not model buildings, but 'remember' drawings as a series of lines.

There are numerous general purpose graphics packages, which if used with a little ingenuity, can produce a limited but acceptable range of architectural drawings. Drafting systems that have been designed specifically for use by architects have either evolved from these or are cut-down versions of systems that have been designed for meticulous engineering applications. Both, which represent extremes of simplicity and complexity, present difficulties to architects. The former is generally easy to use but lacks the ability to create large, exact and complicated related drawings; the cut-down version is generally less 'friendly' but capable of working to minuscule tolerances and high levels of complexity.

Systems which have been tailored for architects overcome the problem with varying degrees of success. In any case, once a system can produce the range of drawings required, its ease and method of use is often a matter of personal preference. Some people prefer mice and 'chummy' menus or icons whilst others are more comfortable with an exacting engineering approach, which generally involves greater use of the keyboard.

An architect is able in theory to produce on an A1 sheet of paper a free-hand sketch, a 1:200 general arrangement drawing, elevations at a different drawn scale, 1:1 details and copious notes. This is by no means impossible using a computer, but the difference is that a sheet of paper can be viewed all at once, and the detail can be read – not so on a 14″ computer screen!

Drawings on a computer require planning and organisation because of the difference between what is stored, what can be seen on a screen, and what can be plotted. Architectural drawings cover a wide range of scaled-down realities, from site plans (1:2500, 1:1250, 1:500) to 1:1 details. The drawing is an exact scale. Computers do not work like that. Dimensions are input in 'real' units; it doesn't matter to the computer whether they are miles, millimetres or British Standard Thumbnails, as long as the input is consistent. For example, a plan of a building which is several thousand units long can be detailed, theoretically down to fractions of a unit, on the same drawing.

If you want to produce drawings more or less in the same way as you do at present but more accurately and with greater consistency, a drafting system is worth considering. An alternative might be a drafting system with 3D visualisation.

Computer-generated drawings tend to look sterile (no wobbly bits and no crossed corners) so at present they are more appropriate for production than presentation drawings – unless, of course, you are able to devise a style of drawing on the computer which is individual and to some extent idiosyncratic.

Although drafting systems produce lines on paper, not a building model, some will allow the input of a third dimension to produce axonometric or isometric projections. A perspective produced by an enhanced drafting system (or a wire-line modeller) is not up to presentation quality but can be used as a base and worked up manually.

A drafting system takes input dimensions as 'real' (full size); drawn scale is specified when a drawing is plotted. The computer is in effect doing a full size drawing, therefore it is possible to put all the necessary detail of a whole building on one plan. This is not a good idea, because when the drawing is plotted at, say, 1:200 the detail will not show, and areas of fine detail will appear as blobs.

Drafting systems have a number of *layers* (levels, views) which can be imagined as sheets of tracing paper. These allow different levels of detail to be put on to separate 'sheets'. Each part of the composite drawing should only have to be input once. For example, a foundation layout can be set up on one layer, steelwork on the next, walls on the next and so on. Areas of a plan that require finer detail can be enlarged and transferred to another layer for detail to be added.

There are considerable differences between drafting systems in methods of input, the ways in which drawings can be constructed, in terminology, limitations to the number and size of drawing files and to the ways in which standard details or symbols can be created and stored.

Sometimes it is more efficient to produce drawings manually, particularly for small complicated jobs. This can only be assessed when users have become familiar with a particular system.

Find out how long it takes to create a drawing. A good draughtsman can work as fast on a drafting system as on a drawing board, some times much faster. A duff manual draughtsman should not be let anywhere near a drafting system – he or she will be even worse and can do much more damage. Drawing on a computer needs an eye firmly connected to a brain and a hand!

A good way for a small practice to start is to install a cheap, micro-based system and use it to produce A4 standard details or general arrangement drawings for standard house types. This will allow people to get the feel of a system, find out what is lacking and know what to look for in a bigger system. (Drawings may be produced via an existing printer, so that buying a plotter at this early stage may be unnecessary – take advice about this.)

Consider carefully what drawings need to be produced and how much duplication there is in the manual draughting methods used in the practice. Both large and small practices must decide whether computer drafting is going to be carried out by means of an office bureau system or whether the aim is to produce an environment where all draughtsmen have a work station. The safe course is to set up a bureau, using two work stations, and see how things go. Provided the original set-up has allowed for potential networking and there is enough space, there should be no problem in extending the system to suit your requirements.

Before starting to look for a system, you will need to know the answers to these questions:

Q. Is the type of work carried out by the practice suited to a drafting system? Is it repetitive work – for hospitals, housing schemes, standard details etc.

Q. What types of drawing need to be produced?

Q. How will the office be organised? How many people will eventually use computer drafting?

What can be expected from a reasonable drafting system?
A drafting system should allow you to draw objects or buildings at the correct size (note: not scale) and in the correct relationship. Drawing is easy on any system, but to draw something specific with exact dimensions is sometimes difficult, particularly if you don't know all the dimensions. Computers work to minuscule tolerances and can't fudge! Lines may be input via the keyboard using absolute, relative or polar co-ordinates, by positioning the cursor at the end points of the line on the screen (difficult to be accurate, even if the cursor co-ordinates are displayed on the screen), or by using a digitising tablet.

There are restrictions on the size and/or number of drawing files that a system can support. This may result in drawings being limited to a maximum number of lines, or limits to the physical size of the real-world objects being represented.

Although computers do not work to a scale, some systems require that the screen is set to a window size or paper size. This means that if you want to draw a building that is 50m long, the screen will be set to represent 60m so that the building fits in. It is always possible to 'zoom in' to enlarge a portion of the drawing, but it is not always possible to zoom out farther than the original setting.

Most systems for technical drawing allow the creation of multiple parallel lines – very useful when drawing cavity walls. Systems that are not designed for architectural use may not 'trim' the last corner.

Hatching methods vary, as does the ease with which hatching can be done. Only closed shapes can be hatched. Problems occur when it is necessary to hatch areas created by the intersection of several lines, curves and polygons. A good test is to see if the area between two non-intersecting differently-sized circles and their external common tangents can be hatched. Hatch may be available in the system as a symbol (this saves memory) but it is then not possible to delete within an area of hatch.

Checklist: Drafting

1 Hardware compatibility

If you are buying software for an existing computer, make absolutely sure that the software will run on it and the memory is adequate. You need a hard disk: it takes a long time to load a drafting system from floppies. If you are investing in a plotter make sure that there is a port for it (or an expansion slot). Will the software drive the plotter (or printer) or do you need an extra board(s)? Similarly can a mouse or tablet be connected? Is there support for a second screen?

Using a drafting system efficiently means using it all the time; it is only sensible to install drafting on an existing microcomputer, which is used for other applications, if you are a one-man-band or, for a larger practice, if you want to try it out. Otherwise buy (or lease) all the hardware and software together.

2 Ease of use

Q. Is input by means of keyboard commands, mouse or digitiser?

Q. Is the system operated by commands, pull-down menus or screen menus?

Q. Are dimensions input from the keyboard? If not, how? Absolute, relative or polar co-ordinates?

Q. Is there 'rubber-banding'?

Q. Is there an on-screen help facility?

Q. Is there an 'oops' or undo command, which overrides the last instruction when you have made a mistake?

Q. How easy is it to locate (or find) and erase (or delete) lines, parts of lines, curves, objects or details (blocks, entities), contents of windows, hatching or symbols? Can this be done selectively or globally?

Q. Can you understand the manual? Is there a quick reference table? Does the manual include a tutorial?

Q. Is it possible to set up grids?

Q. Is it possible to snap to grids? To ends or mid-points of lines? Centres of circles? Anything else?

Q. Is it possible to set up construction lines?

3 Size and speed

Q. Is there a maximum size for a drawing file? What does this limit?

Q. How long does it take to load a drawing file?

Q. How long does it take to redraw a screen?

Q. How long does it take to plot or print a drawing using recommended hardware?

CHECKLIST: DRAFTING

4 Features

Q. How many layers (levels, views) are available?

Q. Is there selective display? Selective plotting? Windowing?

Q. Is it possible to set line style and/or width and/or colour?

Q. Is it possible to draw both single lines and polylines (multilines)? A polyline is one which is drawn continuously to join several points.

Q. Is it possible to draw rectangles, polygons, curves, arcs, circles? How?

Q. Is it possible to draw multiple parallel lines and curves? Nested polygons?

Q. How many hatch styles are available? How easy is it to define areas to be hatched? Is it possible to delete areas of hatch?

Q. Is it possible to copy, multiple-copy, reduce or increase by a scale factor, mirror, rotate, move or drag objects (blocks, entities) or areas of the drawing?

Q. Is dimensioning automatic? Can the the arrow heads be positioned?

Q. How many text fonts and sizes are available? How is text positioned on screen?

Q. Is it possible to extrude from 2D to 3D? Can axonometric or isometric projections be produced?

Q. Are there built in macros? Is it possible to customise using macros?

Q. Is there a library of symbols?

Q. Is there a zoom facility (allows the drawing to be reduced or enlarged on screen)? Within what range?

Q. Is there a pan facility (allows a complete drawing to be moved across the screen)?

Q. Will the software calculate areas?

5 Add-in goodies and links to other software

Some drafting systems have add-in or bolt-on software which allows perspectives to be generated. If this exists, how good is it?

Q. Is it possible to produce a bill of materials?

Q. Are there links to structural or environmental software?

Q. Are there links to databases or spreadsheets?

Q. In what format are drawings output? What format of drawing files can be input (DXF or IGES)?

Q. Is there colour? Can drawings be painted? Shadows?

There should be a variety of line thicknesses, colours and styles (dotted etc). Whether the colour that appears on the screen can be reproduced on the plotter depends on the software and the number of coloured pens in the plotter. In any case, working on a colour screen is much easier than in monochrome; for example, you can set up construction lines in a distinctive colour – in monochrome they are difficult to separate from other lines.

There may be provision for creating windows on the screen in which drawings, possibly from different layers, can be amended or used for reference. The windows can be created at a different screen scale.

It should be possible to select a portion of the drawing and copy, multiple-copy, move, mirror or rotate it, either at the same size or increased or reduced by a scale factor. Most systems will produce dimensions automatically between two indicated points and drawn in a position which must also be indicated by the user. Annotation can be added by entering text via the keyboard and indicating, with the cursor, the desired location on the screen.

Clearly, it is a waste of time to have to input details or symbols that are used frequently (such as door-swings). Some systems contain a library of components which can be rescaled (that is, their real dimensions can be altered) to suit a particular design; they may also allow the creation of new details and symbols either using macros (single 'short cut' commands that represent a series of commands) or parametric programming. *Don't panic!* Devise a test symbol, something like a moulded architrave, and when you are investigating a system ask the demonstrator to show you how long it takes to create, store and retrieve the symbol.

Finally, check how long it takes to regenerate a drawing file or to redraw a screen. Five minutes watching a computer is an eternity! There is no point in stretching or overloading a system. Make sure that the processor is fast enough to cope with the level of complexity that is required.

For modelling systems which allow buildings to be represented in three dimensions and for a variety of attributes to be assigned, the checklist can be taken as that for drafting systems, plus:

---

6 Additions for modelling

Q. Can perspectives be produced as one point, two point and three point?

Q. Can the viewing angle and the eye-height be varied?

Q. Can plans and sections be generated automatically?

Q. Is there hidden line removal?

Q. Is there provision for colour, shadow casting and light-modelling?

Q. Are there links to analysis software for environmental, structural, materials and other performance appraisal?

6.8 Structural and environmental calculations

It is unwise to use a computer program to carry out any calculation that you, or someone in the office, could not carry out 'manually' with the help of a calculator and data tables. It is essential to be able to spot mistakes and unlikely results, particularly in terms of orders of magnitude. An extra zero or a misplaced decimal point can make a big difference!

If you don't know a newton from a joule forget about structural and environmental calculations. Taking into consideration quality assurance, professional indemnity and profit, to name but three, mistakes in calculations are at best time-wasting and a cause of embarrassment; at worst, they may result in building failure or bankruptcy.

Most calculations carried out in architectural practice are based on relatively simple mathematical models which rely on the input of data from extensive tables (for example, steelwork tables, U-values, cost indices etc). Clearly, if this data can be stored and kept up to date, using a computer for calculations can save time and be a powerful tool for testing design solutions. If calculations are infrequently carried out, it may be enough to set up a spreadsheet to cope with them and add new data as necessary. Where complex calculations are a regular feature there may be some suitable software available for the specific tasks. Before making your choice, make sure that it does what you expect it to do. Refer to the checklist opposite.

Finally, it's worth noting that the output from some programs may be acceptable to local authorities in lieu of calculations.

6.9 Office management systems

Office management systems are integrated suites of programs which may include administration, job-running, fees and accounts modules. They may have been developed from integrated packages or by a customised relational database, which may have links to a spreadsheet or wordprocessor.

The choice of a system will depend largely on how well the existing office procedures adapt to the system. Some customisation, particularly in terms of passwords and levels of access, will need to be done, but extensive customisation is costly (at 1989 rates, a minimum of £30 per man hour). It is essential that the user has a clear view of what is

---

Checklist: Structural and environmental calculations

1 Principles
Do you, or does someone in your organisation, understand the principles behind the calculations you want to carry out?

2 Compatibility
Q. Does the software run properly on existing hardware? Is there adequate memory and disk space?
Q. Is the processor fast enough?
Q. Can results be fed into other programs?

3 Ease of use
Q. Are there enough prompts? Does the program explain how, when and why to enter data?
Q. Is it possible to correct a mistake in data entry without having to go back to the beginning of a routine? To correct a mistake retrospectively?
Q. How easy is it to update or add to data tables?

4 Documentation
Q. Does the documentation explain how the program works?
Q. Is there a quick reference guide?

5 Presentation
Q. Is the format in which results are produced acceptable? Is there provision for tables or graphics?

---

required, otherwise customisation can be a long, difficult and acrimonious process – as well as expensive.

Consider at an early stage how many modules will be required immediately and how these may need to be expanded. Usually there is a 'starter kit' which allows users to become familiar with the way the system operates. This may be limited in terms of the number of files and the number and size of the records.

It is essential to decide who is to have access to what, and how access will be limited. Password structures will be set up when the system is installed, but it may also be prudent to set up the system on a machine which can be physically locked.

The system should be installed by the software supplier, who should ensure that everything is up and running. Depending on the cost of the software, some limited 'free' training may be given when the software

---

Checklist: Office management systems

1 Hardware compatibility

If you are starting from scratch, the system should be installed by the software supplier on hardware recommended by the supplier. Make sure that your choice takes into account possible expansion and other applications that you may use in the future.

If the system is being installed on existing hardware make sure that the processor is fast enough, and that there is sufficient memory and disk space.

Q. Do you need a single user or a multi-user system?

Q. Do you require a turnkey system?

2 Size

Make sure you know what information you want to keep in the system.

Q. Are there limitations to the amount of information stored?

3 Ease of use

Q. How easy is it to find your way round the system and to add new records?

Q. Are the on-screen instructions adequate? Help facilities?

Q. How easy is it to spot mistakes?

Q. Does the documentation give clear procedural instructions?

4 Features

Which of the following modules does the software contain (or are they available for future use)?

Administration: staff records, addresses, checklists and diary drawing lists

Job running: project/job files, work in progress, contracts, certificates and instructions, job monitoring

Fees and accounts: cash book, fee details, expenses, salaries and PAYE, job estimating, job analysis, financial forecasting, resource planning, nominal ledger, client (sales) ledger, purchase ledger, invoicing.

5 Customisation

Q. How much customisation is needed?

Q. How many passwords and levels of password can be set up?

Q. What will be the cost of customisation?

6 Training

Q. How much, if any, 'free' training is given? Otherwise, how much does training cost? On whose premises?

Q. How easy is it to get follow-up help? Is there a 'help-line'? How much does further training or 'sorting-out' cost?

is installed, but generally in-house training will cost about £300 per day (at 1989 rates) and about half that figure if it is provided on the software vendor's own premises.

To run a system sensibly and efficiently it should be installed on a dedicated machine which is used solely for administration. The only exception to this is in the case of a very small practice. If you are starting from scratch, obtain the software and the hardware from the same source.

The range of applications that may be provided by a system is covered in the checklist.

6.10 Project management

This is an area where, like calculations, if you don't know how to do it manually, forget it!

In the case of architectural practice it is probable that the facilities provided in an office management system will be more than adequate. There is a great deal of project management software which uses bar charts or critical path analysis. An extensive checklist is unnecessary because it is more than likely that people doing this kind of analysis will be using computers already. Suffice it to say that Pert and Gantt charts can be produced, and these need good graphics. It is essential that an adequate number of resource groups can be accommodated within charts and that the system can cope with the required amount of complexity. In terms of usability, it is also essential to be able to view a chart as a whole to get an overall view – this is not always possible.

Section 7

Implementation

7.1 Choosing hardware

When you have chosen software, you have to make decisions about hardware and whether to buy or lease it. Software suppliers will usually recommend a processor (computer) and first-time users are advised to go along with this choice. If possible, obtain your hardware and software from the same source, whether this is a consultant, supplier or dealer; it makes maintenance easier and you are likely to get a better post-sales service. You will also know whom to blame if the system does not work properly.

Computers are supplied with a monitor and a keyboard, which may be included in the total cost. Check this. For applications other than wordprocessing and calculations a colour screen is essential. High resolution screens (VGA) are recommended for any application which includes graphics. It is increasingly common for these to be supplied with the more expensive computers, but it may be necessary to get a better monitor than the standard model supplied with cheaper machines. 'Cheap and cheerful' computers are not appropriate for anything other than home use or for the one-man-band. (This is because of the limited amount of software available, not necessarily because the machines lack capability.)

The choice of input devices, other than the keyboard, will depend on the software to be run. Again you should base your choice on recommendations from the people who are supplying the software and computer.

When it comes to output devices, particularly printers, there is more scope for personal preference. Depending on your needs, you can opt for any printer which is, or can be made to be, compatible with the computer and software. In the first instance the choice may be determined by cost.

Whatever hardware you buy, or lease, get the best you can afford and take advice. Remember that the initial cost of the hardware is a low proportion of the total cost over a five-year period. Leasing may prove cheaper in real terms than buying. There is no

111

hard-and-fast rule, but the increased total outlay over three years must be weighed against improved service in terms of maintenance and replacement of faulty components. Investigate leasing, and discuss the tax position with your accountant.

A look at the present hardware situation

Only a quick look because it will have changed by the time you read this! The current industry standard is the IBM PC (XT, AT). The corporate power of IBM and market forces dictated that other manufactures adopted this standard and a vast range of clones was produced. Some of these are cheap and nasty and not truly compatible; others are superior to the original product.

Because of the proliferation of the PC and clones, the majority of business and professional software has been developed for these machines. Whilst the PC and PC XT are adequate for some purposes (this book was drafted on an XT clone), they are neither fast nor powerful enough to support some of the latest software. The PC AT (or clone) is the most sensible choice at present for running a wide range of software.

IBM have brought out the PS/2, designed using microchannel architecture (MCA). These machines take 3.5" rather than 5.25" disks. PS/2s can operate under DOS, or the new OS/2 which (like UNIX on larger machines) will support multi-tasking software. (This means that programs can operate in the background while the user works on another program.) It is not clear whether MCA will become the new industry standard.

Apple is one of the several companies who have not followed the PC standard. Users claim that the Apple Macintosh (Mac) range is more user-friendly, has a better user interface and is capable of doing anything a PC (or clone) can, and more. Computer buffs have traditionally considered Macs to be expensive executive toys (probably because they are easy to use), useful only for graphics and publishing. In fact Macs created the market for desktop publishing. Now the situation is changing: despite the fundamental differences in hardware and user interface between PC and Mac, software is being developed for both. Some of the established products for the PC are now available on the Mac. There is also a convergence of Mac and PC styles in the development of a consistent set of user interfaces.

The PC wins on range of software, but the quality of the Macintosh software is as good or better than the PC equivalent.

If you are starting from scratch, do not be dissuaded from investigating Macintosh-based software or indeed software based on other non-standard machines if it seems to fit your needs.

Do not get bogged down trying to make a choice of hardware: pay someone else to do the worrying for you. Technology is changing rapidly; areas to watch are development of low cost work stations, the fate of the PS/2, and machines based on the 80386 and 80486 processors.

You do not need to go for the top end of a range if you do not need it. There is no point in having a Ferrari when all you need is a Fiat Uno.

UPGRADING

Resist any suggestion that you should upgrade the processor of an existing machine. This is not a good idea; better to downgrade the old machine to everyday tasks and buy a new one.

There are several ways of improving the performance of a computer. For example, you could install

- a hard disk
- an extra memory board
- a maths co-processor (speeds up number crunching)
- an accelerator board
- a higher resolution screen

In theory, slotting boards in should be easy – but don't try it! Software may be affected by the changes, and this should be checked out. If you are acquiring new software, take advice from the suppliers about upgrading the hardware. Computers have a limited number of expansion slots and it may be that there is no room for additional boards.

Surely upgrading peripherals should be easy – you just buy one and plug it in? Not so! Apart from the fact the software may not be capable of driving the device, the chances of being able to plug in are low.

WHAT PLUGS INTO WHAT?

Not a lot. There may not be an available port; on a standard machine only one device can be connected through each port. Standard computer 'boxes' have one serial and one parallel port, a video port (to connect the monitor) and possibly a games port. There may be a separate mouse port.

Say you want to connect a scanner, a mouse, a plotter and a printer. The serial plotter is connected to the serial port, the dot matrix printer (parallel) to the parallel port. If there is no mouse port (or connection through the games port) the mouse will have to be connected to a serial port provided by a board in an expansion slot. And the scanner needs a serial port – so it and any subsequent devices will need an expansion slot each. Are there enough expansion slots?

Serial ports are required by modems, digitisers, daisy wheel printers, mice, serial plotters, some laser printers, scanners, and some dongles (security devices).

Parallel ports are required by dot matrix printers, ink jet printers, some laser printers, parallel plotters, some dongles.

All these have a connection lead with a plug on the end. There are at least 25 commonly used plugs, with male and female versions of each. On a PC, for example, the serial port is likely to be an RS232C 25 pin D-type male; the parallel port the same but female, although some ports are 36 pin.

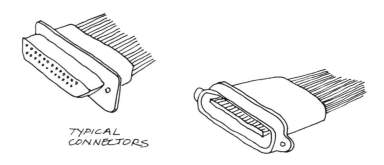

TYPICAL
CONNECTORS

Without going into further detail, it is obvious there may be connection difficulties. For example, dot matrix printers are either fitted with Centronix 36 pin, or perhaps a 25 pin D-type parallel connector, usually male – but not always ...

A HOMILY
The message about hardware is simple: get the best that you can afford, whether bought or leased, all from the same place, and make sure that the supplier is responsible for the whole system. Take advice. Try not to pay for anything until the software is up and running satisfactorily.

7.2 Space and environmental requirements

If you have chosen software and ordered hardware, there will come a day when a number of large cardboard boxes are delivered. The supplier or dealer should install the system – is the office ready for it?

Nowadays, computers do not need special environments, but *people* have much the same needs as ever! Hardware generates heat, computer boxes hum, printers (other than laser) and plotters make a lot of noise, and keyboards make about as much noise as an electric typewriter. Heat should not be a problem unless there is a lot of hardware in a small and poorly ventilated space. Noise can be infuriating. Printers and plotters may need to be acoustically insulated.

Lighting is crucial. It is difficult to work at a VDU if there is disabling glare from either windows or ceiling-mounted luminaires. Whilst a lower level of general illuminance is necessary for work at a computer, it should be possible to vary the illuminance on the plane of any reference material to suit the user. Task lighting is recommended. Blinds should be fitted to windows and VDUs located, where possible, in areas where it is not necessary to keep ceiling-mounted luminaires switched on. It is a good idea to experiment with a TV screen to find the optimum position for a VDU.

Computers require space – much more space than is implied by the glossy sales literature and talk of the 'paperless office'. (Computers that are advertised as having a 'small footprint' take up marginally less desk space than others.)

Any microcomputer needs plenty of space round it for access and to allow for the connection of peripheral devices. The peripherals, which may or may not be on the same surface, also need clear space around them. The VDU will generally be on top of the computer box (some are fixed), but it is an advantage to have a VDU which will swivel horizontally and vertically. The keyboard will normally be attached to the back of the box by a 'spring' cable. Some people like to work with the keyboard on a horizontal surface in front of the VDU, others with the keyboard on their knee or to one side. Mice may be used on the desk surface or on a mouse-pad (200 x 150mm). The space required is about the same for both, but its location will depend on whether the user is right- or left-handed.

Plan the layout of hardware in advance. Don't forget that space is needed for reference material, which should be as nearly as possible the same distance from the eye as the screen, and ideally on an adjustable sloping plane.

The manuals provided with hardware and software require shelf space; a two metre run is usually adequate. Although reference to manuals will become increasingly less frequent, they should be within easy reach of the operator.

Where applications are to be used which require the computer

115

operator to work at a wordprocessor or drafting system all day, the environmental conditions and the furniture layout should be considered for every individual.

Furniture layout

- The desk and chair should be arranged so that the centre of the screen is 5 to 20 degrees below the horizontal eyeline. This also applies to the support for reference material that has to be read.

- The working plane should be large enough to enable the user to reposition the 'electronic tools' according to the nature of the work.

- The layout should respond to the user's reach. An L-shaped or curved desk might allow equipment and reference material to be reached more easily.

- The underside of the desk should be high enough to give plenty of knee clearance. Choose desks whose height can be adjusted to suit individual users.

- Large digitisers must be positioned carefully. It is difficult to use them from a seated position. To avoid 'draughtsman's back' problems, the digitiser may need to be raised or tilted.

- Chairs should give firm lumbar support; this can be provided by an adjustable back rest. They should be stable (five point base with self-locking casters), have a swivel action and adjustable seat height. Where keyboards are in constant use it is more comfortable for the operator if the chair seat slopes slightly downwards toward the back support (<14degrees).

Electricity

Trailing cables are dangerous, unsightly and bad for the image! Wire-managed furniture is now commonplace in large commercial offices, but it is not necessary where the computer installation consists of a couple of micros.

Computers require 'clean' electricity (see 7.4); surges or power drops can cause damage to both hardware and software and result in the loss of data. Networked microcomputers and minicomputers should be on a separate protected circuit to avoid interference from other office machinery. For microcomputers it is sufficient to feed the computer and peripherals from a multi-socket block with a built-in filter. The block can be fixed to the back of the desk and the single cable from it to the power supply can be made safe and unobtrusive. All equipment should be properly earthed.

Computers and people are adversely affected by static. This can be prevented by using an anti-static floor covering and maintaining a relative humidity of 50 to 60%.

7.3 Installation and maintenance

The hardware should be set up by the supplier, who should install the operating system, test it, and ensure that the peripherals work properly.

For most applications the installation of software is relatively simple; it should be done by the person in the office who will be responsible for the computer and who should have a working knowledge of the operating system.

Where software has been tailored to suit individual needs, installation will be included in the cost. Where some element of in-house training is included in the software, it is usual for the person providing the training to set up the system.

Setting up databases and complicated spreadsheet applications is time-consuming and exacting. It is not simply a case of loading the software and running it, but of getting the system into a condition which will allow it to be used in the desired way.

Password protection and levels of access need to be set up, and there may be a need for a customised 'front end' (what you see and what instructions you are given when the computer is switched on). It is sensible and cost-effective to employ someone, probably a consultant, to do this for you.

Maintenance
Maintenance for hardware will cost about 15% of the capital outlay per annum. It is essential to take out a maintenance contract and to read the small print. Most suppliers and dealers undertake to trouble-shoot the same working day as a complaint is received or, at worst, within 24 hours. The service may be slightly better if the hardware is leased, as faulty equipment is generally replaced immediately.

For software, other than for bespoke systems, maintenance is likely to consist of updates as they occur and access to a 24-hour help-line. Help is not going to appear on the doorstep simply because you are unable to use the system. Even if you are convinced that the software is faulty, it is unlikely that there will be any help available other than from a reporting service. For this reason it is essential that the software is installed correctly at the outset and that training has been provided by someone who can demonstrate that it works properly.

7.4 Safety and security

Employees are covered by the *Health and Safety at Work Act (1974)*. Computers do not normally constitute a health hazard if they are properly set up. Suggestions of danger from excessive radiation from VDUs are unproven, but there are much more straightforward dangers. Electric shocks can occur from the build-up of static, from faulty wiring and connections and from overloaded power sockets. People can trip over trailing cables.

Other detrimental effects are caused by inadequate consideration of the ergonomics in relation to the furniture and the environment. A comfortable temperature, adequate humidity to avoid static, adequate ventilation, careful positioning of anything that generates noise, and lighting that does not give rise to glare or screen reflections are all essential. The design of the work place is vitally important. Work surfaces, desks and chairs should be chosen so that the keyboard and other input devices can be used with the hands, arms and shoulders in the correct position.

People who work continuously at computers should take regular breaks, at least once an hour, to give their muscles and tendons time to relax. Repetitive stress injury (RSI) is an increasingly common and recognised complaint, particularly amongst keyboard operators. It is tiring to peer at a screen for long periods, and here again the eye muscles need to relax by focusing on a distant view (>12m). Operators should not be discouraged from looking out of the window!

Headaches can be caused by a combination of unsuitable lighting, poor ventilation, screen flicker, boredom, stress or general dislike of computers. If people think they are getting headaches because of a computer, they might be better employed doing something else unless the specific cause can be identified and removed or mitigated.

There is no reason why working with a keyboard should be any more likely to cause RSI than working at a typewriter, except that people tend to work faster and in a more static position. Similarly, using a digitiser should be no worse for the back and neck muscles than working at a drawing board. If the technology is new to a practice, and problems occur, the new set-up will be blamed. If people can move around frequently and avoid working in one position, problems should not occur. It is important to note early symptoms such as tiredness, pins and needles, weakness, swelling joints, and nagging pains in the wrists, arms, shoulders, neck or back. Take them seriously and ensure that medical advice is obtained.

Disasters and theft
What happens in the event of fire, flood or burglary? Not only will you lose the hardware and some software, but a considerable amount of data. The possibility of a disaster should be considered. Back-up (and preferably double back-up) of all data should be made at least once a day, and one copy should be kept in a separate place (another office, a partner's house, a safe deposit box).

Hardware should be insured under a business machines all risks policy. If equipment has been delivered but not invoiced, is on loan or on trial, it should be insured to cover its value as 'goods held in trust'. Insurance arrangements for leased equipment should be discussed with the lessor.

It is not usually worth insuring software unless it has been developed in-house or is bespoke. However, where it can be copied but can only be run when using a security disk or a plug-in dongle, the dongle should be insured for its full replacement value. Software companies are reluctant to replace lost dongles unless there is absolute proof of destruction.

Data insurance is expensive and can be difficult to assess. Back-up copies are often a better form of insurance than taking out a policy against physical damage. Insurance against theft should be considered if the data would be valuable to another party.

Power problems
Glitches, brown-outs and *outages* are jargon for spikes, voltage drop and power failure. Glitches are created when nearby electrical equipment is switched on and off. Drops in voltage of the mains supply are rare in the UK, but a frequent occurrence in other parts of the world.

High frequency energy in glitches can pass through the regulator mechanism of a computer and can cause temporary failure of software, loss of data, corruption of disks and, worst of all, can throw the chip into disarray, causing it to overheat and self-destruct. Glitches can be overcome by installing a filter on the mains plug or lead. A more expensive but more effective solution is line conditioning boxes. These contain filters and actively controlled circuits. High energy is filtered out and compensation can be made for brown-outs where the mains voltage drops for some time. An effective earth on the mains is a prerequisite for the success of any filter.

Where computers are used all the time (particularly where data is sensitive – military, medical, financial etc) an uninterrupted power supply (UPS) may be necessary. If the power goes down, everything in active memory is lost. This reinforces the importance of regular back-up. If loss of mains power would cause irreparable damage to your practice a UPS should be considered. This can be provided by a battery that is continuously charged from the mains. Equipment to provide ten minutes of operating time for a 300 to 1,000W installation costs about as much as a microcomputer. A 2.5kW supply, which would support a network of PCs or a minicomputer for thirty minutes, costs about £4,000.

Computers can suffer from electrical interference from inside or outside the building. If the cause is not identifiable the Electricity Board should be asked to investigate. Computers can cause interference to other equipment, particularly radios. There may also be problems when several machines are linked by data lines and signals can be transmitted to nearby cables.

Access to computers and data
The simplest way of reducing the risk of theft and unauthorised access to computer equipment is to lock it up. This is impractical for installations in large open offices, but equipment can be fixed to desk tops, and alarm systems installed. All areas containing computer equipment should be security locked.

Unauthorised use within an organisation can be discouraged by using machines which can be physically locked, and by making individual users responsible for the key. But what is to stop that innocent-looking office junior (male or female, remember) from copying software or browsing through data files in the lunch hour? Not a lot, if machines are on open access. The only defence is careful password protection for entry. Users are often careless about passwords, blithely writing them down for all to see. Passwords should be confidential and changed frequently.

If the installation is large enough, there will be someone who manages it. The impeccable discretion of such persons should not be taken for granted. They will have the knowledge and skill to gain access to anything on the system. Confidential information should not

120

be kept on a hard disk or on a networked machine; it should be saved on floppy disks and locked in a safe with a back-up copy elsewhere.

Networks should be set up in a way that makes it difficult to corrupt data on other machines or to interfere with other users.

Systems which are linked to the outside world by a modem with an auto-answering facility are vulnerable to hackers and require password protection. If possible, the system should be disconnected from the modem out of working hours.

Software and data

Software and data are at risk from malicious and accidental damage, theft and 'viruses'. It is impossible to devise protective measures against malicious damage other than taking the normal security precautions. Destruction can occur when there is a disk failure, a head-crash, an electrical surge, or when the DELETE *.* or FORMAT commands are used improperly. Keep two copies of everything!

Software may be copy-protected, may require a security disk or dongle to run it, or neither. Copying software is theft and should be actively discouraged. Everyone does it on the quiet but, moral considerations apart, it is risky since the advent of the computer 'virus'.

Viruses

Viruses are destructive programs which attach themselves to a file used frequently by the operating system. They can be passed on to other disks and directories by the DIR command. They can cause immediate destruction of the disk data structure, or can associate with the clock and lurk until a specific date. They are capable of self-reproduction. They are 'caught' from disks of dubious origin or unauthorised copies of software. They are not always apparent and can be disguised as harmless files. Regular checks should be made of the directories to see if the size of anything has inexplicably increased – if it has, your computer has probably contracted an anti-social disease. There are cleansing programs available, but there is usually no cure!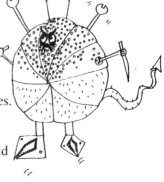

Software and disks should not be used unless they arrive intact in their pristine packages. Employees should be warned against bringing disks 'borrowed from a friend' to try out on the office machines. Everyone, including you, should be wary of 'free' software.

Floppy disks

If two copies of everything are to be kept on floppy disks, there will have to be adequate indexing and storage facilities. A floppy disk is easy to steal. Disks should be kept in containers which are dust-proof and, if necessary, fire-proof. Disks can be damaged by heat, moisture, magnetic fields (generated by telephones and electrical equipment), friction, airport scanners, shop security barriers and general mis-handling.

Data Protection Act

The *Data Protection Act 1984* legislates against unauthorised disclosure of information about individuals which is kept on a computer. It is permissible to keep personal details of employees for accounting (salary) purposes. Where information (other than addresses) is kept about clients, contractors etc, it is necessary to register under the Act. Individuals have the right of access to information held about them.

Details of registration and the necessary forms can be obtained from the Office of the Data Protection Registrar, currently at Springfield House, Water Lane, Wilmslow, Cheshire SK9 5AX (tel: 0625 535777 and 0625 525711). At present (1989) the fee is £56 for three years registration.

Section 8

Conclusions

8.1 The end or the beginning?

If you are a first-time user you should conduct a rigorous examination of office procedures before acquiring a computer to run any application other than wordprocessing. Small practices should start at this level. Large practices, if there are any remaining that are not using computers, should employ a consultant or appoint an in-house expert.

Wordprocessing is safe and cost-effective. Any of the well-known packages will be adequate for general use but you should check which printers the software is capable of driving as it is the printer which will determine the quality of the output. If other applications are being considered, make sure that files from the wordprocessor can be accepted by other software.

The minimum standard for hardware for professional use is a 80286 processor (IBM PC-AT or clone, or equivalent Macintosh), 30Mb hard disk, 640k memory and a VGA screen. Anything less will not run efficiently the spreadsheet, management or drafting software that you may want to use. Much newly developed software needs a 80386 (or equivalent) based machine with greater memory to run at its best.

A machine supporting a wordprocessor can be used immediately for secretarial purposes and can be used to enable people in the office to become keyboard-literate and familiar with the operating system and the directory and file structure. It is a good idea to invest in some cheap software for training purposes. A filer, a spreadsheet and a rudimentary drafting system can be obtained for under £100 each. These will be of limited use, but will give you enough experience to know what to look for in a bigger system. You would have to pay about £300 for ten hours of professional tuition.

If you are not a first-time user, make a clean start. Existing hardware can be used for wordprocessing, written-off or sold. New software and hardware should be bought together.

8.2 Watchpoints

- Don't rush into a High Street shop and buy a computer.
- Decide what you want to do.
- Decide how much money is available, and consider software, hardware, furniture, training, maintenance and running costs.
- Decide what applications you need.
- Locate software that seems suitable and see it in operation on the specific type of application that you want, not just a slick demonstration. (This is particularly important when choosing a drafting system. Dealers are usually more tuned in to the needs of engineers than architects.)
- Check that there is provision for training and maintenance.
- Make sure there is enough space in the office to accommodate the computer, that the environmental conditions and furniture are suitable and that there is a clean electricity supply.
- Get the best hardware you can afford, and make sure that it will support the software you intend to use comfortably, and that it can be extended or expanded easily. Get the dealer to set up hardware and peripherals, and install the operating system and software that you have bought from the same source.
- Investigate leasing as well as buying.
- Do not acquire any hardware less than the equivalent of an 80286 processor, 30Mb hard disk, 640k memory and VGA screen.
- Check hardware maintenance contracts and call-out time.
- Unless you are a one- or two-man-band do not mix widely differing applications on one machine. The following combinations are acceptable: wordprocessing and management, wordprocessing and DTP. Drafting should be by itself.

The computer scene is changing all the time. Watch out for developments in these areas:

- software
- low cost work stations for drafting (RISC technology)
- better than VGA resolution and display technology
- 80386 and 80486 machines
- Apple
- IBM
- manufacture of 'better' clones
- windows environments that work!

- multi-tasking
- user interfaces

Computers *count*. They can be immensely useful, fast and accurate – or idiosyncratic, boring and tedious. They are not really alarming, they are just tools. Remember what they say about bad workmen?

Good luck!

Glossary

Address
Location where data is stored in memory.

ALGOL
A programming language for scientific applications.

Algorithm
A series of instructions for solving specific problems.

Alphanumeric
Relating to letters of the alphabet and numeric digits 0–9.

ALU
Arithmetic and Logic Unit. The part of the processor that does the 'thinking' and counting.

Analogue (analog)
A smoothly changing physical state which can be used to measure another (like the hands on a clockwork watch).

Animation
Making moving pictures.

Applications software
Software produced to carry out specific tasks.

ASCII
American Standard Code for Information Interchange. Has 256 unique identifiers for alphanumeric symbols.

Assembly language
A low level language which converts a programming language to machine code.

Back-up
Copies of software and data kept for security purposes.

BASIC
Beginners' All-purpose Symbolic Instruction Code. The most commonly used programming language for non-specialist applications.

Baud-rate
The rate at which data is transmitted between computers, using a modem, measured in bits per second. V21 is 300 baud, V22 is 1200 baud, V22bis is 2400 baud.

Batch
Data which is processed in one go.

Binary system
A number system based on powers of two, and using two digits, 0 and 1.
For example 10 in binary $= 2^1 = 2$ in decimal; $1000 = 2^3 = 8$.

Bit
Binary digit

8 bit, 16 bit, 32 bit
An indication of the speed of the processor. The higher the faster.

Bit-map

A way of transferring images (pictures) which gives a description of every pixel (picture element) on the screen.

Block

A group of data items or instructions transferred as a whole; (wordprocessing and DTP) a piece of text identified and in one format; (drafting) a group of entities.

Board

A circuit board or card on which computer components are mounted. Extra boards can be added to the expansion slots in a computer to improve storage or performance.

Brown-out

A voltage drop in mains electricity.

Buffer

A small memory which acts as temporary storage space, associated with peripheral devices.

Bug

A fault in software or hardware that causes things to go wrong.

Bundled software

Software sold with and included in the price of hardware.

Bus

A route along which data is passed within the computer.

Byte

Eight bits.

C

A programming language commonly used in conjunction with the UNIX operating system.

CAAD

Computer Aided Architectural Design.

CAD

Computer Aided Design (usually applied to drafting and modelling).

Card

See *Board*.

Cassette

A data storage medium similar to an audio-cassette. May be acceptable for home computers, otherwise slow and inappropriate.

Cell

A unique area of a spreadsheet where data, text or formulae can be inserted.

Centronics

A proprietary name for a commonly used connector. A parallel interface.

CGA

Colour Graphics Adapter. The first colour graphics standard produced by IBM for screens used with the PC.

Character

The smallest addressable block of information processed as a unit. Usually 8 bits.

Chip

A small slice of silicon which holds a printed circuit.

CICA

Construction Industry Computer Association. An independent consultancy based in Cambridge.

Clock
A quartz crystal whose oscillations control the speed at which the central processor operates.

Clone
A copy of a computer that is meant to be exact and 100% compatible.

COBOL
COmmon Business Oriented Language. A programming language for business applications.

Code
The activity of coding; a defined set of bit patterns.

Column
A vertical column of cells on a spreadsheet; a vertical column of text in wordprocessing or DTP.

Communications
The means by which computers can communicate remotely.

Compatibility
The ability of computer systems to work together; the ability to transfer data from one computer or peripheral to another.

Compiler
A program which converts high level languages into machine code.

Consultant
Someone who professes computer expertise and is paid for a service.

Control unit
The part of the central processing unit which controls its operations.

Co-processor
An extra board added to speed up the computer's performance.

Copy
A function in computer software which allows software, text, drawings or files to be replicated.

CP/M
Control Program for Microcomputers. One of the operating systems commonly found on 8-bit machines.

CPS
Characters per second. The rate at which printers print.

CPU
Central Processing Unit. The part of the computer which does the 'thinking'. Contains a control unit, arithmetic and logic unit, ROM and RAM. Usually mounted on a 'motherboard'.

Cursor
Cross-hairs or a flashing mark on a screen which enables points to be located.

Cut and paste
A term used in wordprocessing and DTP. Deleting blocks of a document and inserting them elsewhere.

2D
2-dimensional. Applied to drafting systems.

3D
3-dimensional. Applied to modelling systems.

Daisy wheel
A type of printer where letters are produced by the impact of characters arranged around the spokes of a wheel against a ribbon. Produces letter quality output, but no graphics.

129

Data
Information in digital form.

Database
An electronic filing system which allows files to be cross-referenced and searched.

Data glove
An input device which allows hand movements to be digitally encoded.

Data helmet
An input device which allows eye movements to be digitally encoded.

Data Protection Act
Legislation under which computer users should register if they are keeping personal details of individuals on a computer system.

DBMS
Database Management System. Software which allows a database to be set up and operated.

Debug
Search and destroy bugs! Programs are available to do this.

Denary
The decimal numeric notation – the one with which we are all familiar.

DIF
Data Interchange Format. A format which allows data to be transferred between different databases.

Digital
Consisting of or operating with binary digits.

Digitiser
A flat tablet which allows digital transfer of drawings (vectors) to a computer.

Directory
A collection of files on a computer system.

Disk (not 'disc')
A storage device. Data are recorded in magnetised spots on concentric rings, called tracks.

Disk drive
A mechanism for reading data on disks.

Dongle
A device to stop software (programs) being used by unauthorised people. Dongles may be plugged into one of the computer ports, may be a security disk, or some other device.

Dot matrix
A type of printer where characters are formed by impact, by heat, or electrostatically from an arrangement of pins.

Drum plotter
A plotter, usually A1 or A0, where the paper rotates over a drum.

DTP
Desk top publishing. Software which allows for pages of set-up text in a variety of fonts and points, and for the insertion of illustrations.

Drafting system
A computer system for draughting.

Duplex
Duplex data transmission between computers means that data can be transmitted in both directions simultaneously.

DXF
Drawing eXchange Format. A standard for the transfer of drawing files.

EGA
Enhanced Graphics Adapter, the improved version of CGA. Gives a screen resolution of (typically) 640 x 350 and an enhanced palette of colours.

Entity
A file in some databases; a drawing element in some drafting and modelling systems.

Expert system
A program which allows a body of information to be built up within a system which can then be interrogated logically.

Field
Area of data within a record (database terminology); category of information. For example, Mabel Jones might be in a field called 'name' on a record in a database called 'first-time users.'

File
A collection of related data, used for reference or processing.

Fixed-point notation
Numbers are expressed as digits with the decimal point in the correct place, eg 162.34673. The number of digits handled in fixed-point notation is limited by the computer. See also *Floating-point notation*.

Filer
An electronic card index which contains a number of records (cards) and can be searched by field (category of information required).

Film recorder
Camera-like device for producing photographic slides with accurate colour rendering of a screen image.

Firmware
Software that is built into a computer.

Flat bed plotter
A plotter on which a number of pens produce drawings on a horizontal sheet of paper. Sizes vary from A3 to A0.

Floating-point notation
(scientific notation) Numbers are expressed as a fractional value (mantissa) followed by an integer exponent of the base. For example, 472100 could be expressed as 0.4721×10^6, or 0.4721 E6. This enables very large numbers to be expressed with a limited number of digits. Clearly there is some loss of precision. See also *Fixed-point notation*.

Floppy disk
A storage medium used by microcomputers and minicomputers. Disks are commonly 3", 3.5", 5.25" and 8", single- or double-sided, single or double density. They must be the correct size and formatted for use on a specific computer.

Flow chart
A chart which shows the logical sequence of processes or events. Used in programming and in project management.

Font
A style and size of lettering, eg Times 12pt, Meridien 9pt (here) etc.

Footprint
The space computer kit takes up.

Format

The way data is organised; the process of organising a disk so that it can be read by a particular computer. Reformatting it will destroy all existing data.

FORTRAN

FORmula TRANslation. A programming language for scientific applications.

Gantt chart

A bar chart which shows the relationship between tasks and timescales. Used in project management.

GEM

Digital Research's Graphic Environment Manager. Uses screen menus and icons.

Glitch

A surge or spike on the mains electricity supply which may cause loss or corruption of data in active memory.

Graphics

Drawing and production of pictures (rather than drafting).

Greeking

Contracting letters on a reduced screen view so that they become illegible but show page layout.

Hacker

An expert and fanatical person whose hobby it is to gain access to other people's computers. Usually harmless unless careless, but can be malicious or criminal.

Hard copy

Paper copies of data that has been produced on a computer.

Hard disk

A non-removable disk inside the computer. 30Mb is the most common. Disks up to 640Mb are available.

Hardware

All the computer kit.

Head

A read/write device for transferring data to and from a disk. Analogous to a pick-up on a record player.

Head-crash

A mechanical/electronic head failure, where the read/write head damages a disk or corrupts data on it.

Hertz

A measure of frequency measured in cycles per second. Used as a measure of clock speed.

Hex

Hexadecimal notation. Numbers are expressed to a base of 16: 1,2,3,4,5,6,7,8,9,A,B,C,D,E,F,10 etc. For example, 11 in hex is 17 in denary; 100 hex is $16^2 = 256$ denary. This notation is useful in computer programming.

High-level language

An English-like programming language.

IBM

International Business Machines.

IBM compatible

A computer which should be able to run the same software as an IBM PC. However IBM now has several standards other than the 8086 machine.

Software produced for 80286, 80386 machines and the new PS/2 range is not usually downwardly compatible.

Icon

A graphic symbol used to indicate a menu option on a screen (VDU) activated by the selection of the icon with the cursor.

IGES

International Graphic Exchange Standard. A standard format for the transfer of drawing files.

Information

Anything with a defined meaning.

Ink jet

A printer where characters are formed by jets of ink. These may be coloured. The more expensive models are capable of reasonable colour representation.

Input device

A device for converting information to digital signals.

Integer

A whole number.

Integrated circuit

An electronic circuit about the size of a pin head, transferred by chemical and physical means to the surface of a silicon chip.

Integrated design system

A suite of interactive programs allowing a range of drafting, modelling and forecasting.

Integrated package

A software package combining several different applications: commonly wordprocessing, database, spreadsheet, graphics and communications.

Interface

A boundary, physical or logical, between two physical or logical systems. For example, man and computer; plug and socket.

Interference

Electrical or magnetic fluctuations, or radio signals disturbing the proper operation of a computer; signals caused by a computer that disturb other electrical equipment.

Interpreter

A program which translates a high level language, line by line, to machine code during the course of operation.

Joystick

An input device which allows movement of a control through 360 degrees. Used for computer games.

K

Kilo = 1000; in computing K (kilobyte) = 1024 bytes (2^{10}).

Kerning

(DTP terminology) Spacing between letters to allow for kerns (the bits that stick out from letters, serifs etc) so that the letters appear to fit closely.

Keyboard

The most common input device. Resembles a typewriter keyboard with extra, often programmable, function keys.

LAN

Local area network. Computers that are physically joined together on the same or neighbouring sites.

Languages

Sets of grammar, syntax and rules which convert instructions in spoken or written language to digital information.

Laser disk

A high capacity storage disk which is read using a laser.

Laser printer

A printer which produces one page at a time. The quality of output (300 dots per inch) is currently better than other printers.

Layer

A 'sheet of tracing paper' on a drafting system (known also as a level or view).

Library

Stored, organised information or data.

Light pen

A device for locating points on the screen of a VDU.

Machine code

Binary code; the lowest level language.

Macro

A program that reduces a commonly used series of instructions to a single command.

Mail merge

(wordprocessing terminology) A way of producing standard letters with varying paragraphs, eg addresses.

Mainframe

A big computer supporting many users who share data.

Maintenance

The upkeep of hardware and software. Will probably cost 15% of the capital cost per annum.

Mbyte

Megabyte = 2^{20} bytes.

MCA

MicroChannel Architecture. A new internal design used by IBM in its PS/2 range.

Memory

The 'space' in the computer where problems are handled and solved, RAM. The contents of this active memory are lost when the computer is switched off. May apply to the capacity of storage devices.

Menu

Items or commands shown on a screen for selection by a cursor or key-stroke.

Microcomputer

A stand-alone computer. Microcomputers cannot share data unless networked.

Microprocessors

8088, 8086, 80286, 80386, 80486 PC microprocessors are available. The 8086 and 8088 are used with 'standard' PCs. The others are faster and are capable of accessing more memory. The higher the number, the faster they can go.

Minicomputer

A computer which can share data and which can support a number of users.

Modem
MOdulator/DEModulator. A communications device which allows transfer of digital data to analogue signals on telephone lines, in order to facilitate communications between computers.

Motherboard
The board within the computer on which the CPU components are mounted.

Mouse
A pointing device which moves the screen cursor in relation to its movement on a horizontal surface.

MS-DOS
MicroSoft Disk Operating System. An operating system.

Multifinder
A multi-user operating system used on the Apple Macintosh.

Multi-tasking
The ability to have several programs loaded and running on a computer at one time.

Multi-user
A computer system that can be used by more than one user at the same time.

NCC
National Computer Centre. Independent consultants, based in Manchester.

Network
Linked computers.

Notation
Ways of representing numbers.

On-line
Directly connected to a computer system.

Operating system
Program or programs by means of which the method of operation of a computer is organised. It is usually bought with the computer and installed by the supplier.

Optical character recognition
An input device where typed or hand-written characters are scanned and identified.

Orphan
(DTP terminology) A line of text or a word, isolated at the bottom of a page, that belongs to a paragraph on the next page. See also *Widow*.

OS/2
An operating system developed by IBM to run on 80286(AT) and 80386 based machines. Will support multi-tasking.

Outage
A mains power failure.

Output
Data which comes out of a computer.

Output device
A piece of equipment which converts digital data from a computer to a form which is understandable. This may be transitory on a VDU, stored on a disk, or produced as hard copy.

Paddle
An input device used for computer games.

Page description language
Software used by laser printers to describe a full page of illustrations and text.

Paint
The ability to colour areas of the screen selectively.

Parallel
Data transference 8 bits at a time.

Parallel port
A plug or socket which allows data transference in parallel.

Parity
(communications terminology) An error check when data is transferred. An extra bit is added to each character in binary notation so that the sum of the '1's in the string is always even or always odd.

Pascal
A programming language named after Blaise Pascal.

Path
The route from the top directory of a computer via sub-directories to a file.

PC
Personal computer.

PC-DOS
The IBM version of MS-DOS. An operating system.

PERT
(project management terminology) Program Evaluation and Review Technique. A PERT chart is used for project planning and critical path analysis.

Peripheral
Hardware devices connected to a computer.

Pitch
(wordprocessing and DTP) The spacing of printed characters.

Pixel
Picture element. One of the dots which make up a screen image.

Point
(wordprocessing and DTP) The size of a printed character.

Primitive
(drafting and modelling) One of the basic elements from which a drawing or model is built up.

Printer
An output device which can produce text and/or graphics.

Processor
The 'chip' that does the 'thinking'.

Program
A set of instructions for a computer.

Programming language
A code to convert a logical problem to one which can be handled by a computer.

Proportional spacing
(DTP) Spacing between characters that allows for the width of each letter.

PS/2
IBM's new range of personal computers using micro channel architecture and intended to support the OS/2 operating system.

Public domain
Software that may be distributed freely. Should be used with care as it is an easy way to spread viruses.

Quality Assurance
Criteria set out in BS 5750. A management process to provide reasonable assurance that the services or product to be provided are in accordance with predetermined standards, and will reach set standards.

QWERTY
Standard keyboard layout in English-speaking countries.

RAM
Random Access Memory. Measured in kilobytes or megabytes, eg 640k for a PC. Resides on a series of chips. Active memory which determines the size of program that can be handled and which disappears when the computer is switched off.

Raster
A type of screen display when the screen is scanned many times per second.

Real time
Data is processed immediately, or for however long it takes, so that output can be provided which will influence subsequent input.

Record
(database) An individual 'card' in an electronic card index.

Resolution
The number of pixels on a screen. The greater the number, the better the resolution.

RISC
Reduced Instruction Set Computer. Generic term used to describe a range of powerful computer chips.

Roller ball
An input device used for moving a screen cursor.

ROM
Read Only Memory. Chips which contain pre-set data, which control the internal operation of a computer.

RS232
A commonly used serial interface.

Scale
(drafting and modelling) Input to computers is in real, full-size, dimensions. Scale refers to the increase or decrease of apparent screen scale, or to the scale at which a drawing is plotted.

Scanner
An input device for converting pictures and photographs to digital data.

Screen
The television-like device that lets you see what's going on.

Scientific notation
See *Floating-point notation.*

Security disk
A dongle. A floppy disk that must be inserted into a floppy disk drive to run software.

Serial
Data transmission bit by bit.

Serial port
A plug or socket which allows serial data transmission.

Shareware
Public domain software.
Shelfware
Software that has been bought and rarely, if ever, used.
Snap
(drafting) The ability to lock on to features of drawings.
Software
Programs of instructions that tell a computer what to do.
Solid modelling
(modelling) Modelling in which solid objects are defined, and physical attributes can be assigned to them.
Spreadsheet
Software which allows text, numbers and formulae to be entered in a matrix of 'cells' and then manipulated. Good for 'what-if' calculations.
Stand-alone
A computer that is not connected to another.
Storage
Means of storing programs and data, commonly hard or floppy disk.
Surface model
A model which is composed of infinitely thin planes. Used for visualisation.
Tablet
A digitiser.
Tape
A storage medium.
Tape-streamer
A high capacity back-up storage device.
Terminal
A VDU and keyboard linked to a multi-user computer.
Thermal printer
A dot matrix printer which requires heat-sensitive paper.
Toggle
A switch used to flip between functions on a computer.
Touch screen
An input device. Touching the VDU screen can be used for the selection of menu items.
Tracker-ball
An input device similar to a roller-ball.
Turnkey
A computer or computer system dedicated to one use.
Updates
Software developments provided under a maintenance contract.
UNIX
A multi-tasking operating system.
User-friendly
An interface which gives the user instructions.
Vapourware
Software which resides in the brain of a systems analyst or programmer (and for which you are waiting!).
VDU
Visual display unit.

Vector
A line defined by length and direction. Output from drafting systems is by definition of vectors, ie the co-ordinates of the beginning and end points of lines.

VGA
Video Graphics Array. Becoming the standard for screen resolution. Commonly 640 x 480 using from 16 to 256 colours.

View
May mean simply a view of an object, or may mean a layer or level in drafting and modelling terminology.

Virtual memory
Where there is not enough memory in RAM for a program's needs, it may use parts of the hard disk as virtual memory, exchanging data between memory and disk as necessary.

Virus
A destructive program which attaches itself to a file frequently used by the operating system. Contagious and self-replicating, and can be 'caught' from unauthorised software and from floppy disks of dubious origin.

Visualisation
(modelling or enhanced drafting) Programs that allow models to be viewed from many directions.

Voice recognition
A development area for input devices that can recognise human speech patterns.

Widow
(DTP terminology) A line of text or a word, isolated at the top of a page, that belongs to a paragraph on the preceding page. See also *Orphan*.

WIMP
Window Icon Mouse Pull-down-menu, or Window, Icon, Menu, Pointing-device, or Window Icon Mouse Pointer. They mean the same thing: an attempt to produce a user-friendly interface. Often applied to graphic environments like Microsoft Windows and Digital Research GEM.

Window
(drafting and modelling) A variable size box on the screen which can be used to select portions of drawing for editing, or an area of the screen where another program can be run at the same time as the main program.

Winchester disk
A hard disk.

Wire-line model
(modelling) A 3D model built up of lines representing the intersection of planes.

Work station
A computer dedicated to fast graphics, drafting and/or modelling.

WYSIWYG
What You See (on the screen) Is What You Get (on the printer).

Bibliography and Further Reading

Hardware and software

Using Microcomputers: Applications for Business
    Spence and Windsor
    The Times Mirror/Mosby, St Louis 1987
Revise Computer Studies
    Tony Rackham
    Charles Letts & Co Ltd, London 1985
Input Devices
    Edited by Sol Sherr
    Academic Press New York and London 1988

Assessing needs

Quality Assurance
    RIBA Journal *Practice* Supplements September and November 1988
Writing Matters
    Alaine Hamilton
    Professional Communication series, RIBA Publications, London 1989

Applications

BUSINESS AND MANAGEMENT
Using Microcomputers: Applications for Business
    Spence and Windsor
    The Times Mirror/Mosby St Louis 1987
A Personal Guide to Personal Computing
    Geoff Wheelwright
    Quiller Press, London 1987
Essentials of Computer Data Files
    Owen Hanson
    Pitman Publishing Inc., London 1985

DRAFTING AND MODELLING
Computer Aided Design in Refurbishment
    John Kronenburg
    The Estates Gazette Ltd, London 1987

Microcomputer Aided Design for Architects
  Gerhard Schmitt
  John Wiley & Sons Ltd, New York 1988
Teach Yourself Computer Graphics
  John Lansdown
  Hodder & Stoughton, London 1987

COMMUNICATIONS
The Hacker's Handbook III
  Hugo Cornwell
  Century Hutchinson Ltd, London 1988

SAFETY AND SECURITY
The Hacker's Handbook III (see above)
Visual Display Unit Workplace: Emerging Trends and Problems
  European Foundation for the Improvement of Living and Working
  Conditions, 1986

General

RIBA Computer Surveys 1983 and 1988
RIBAJ Journal 'Practice' Supplement January 1988

Managing with Computers
  Terry Rowan
  Pan Business Management, London 1982
Introducing Computers
  Malcolm Peltu
  NCC, Manchester 1983
Computer Aided Architectural Design
  William J Mitchell
  VNR, New York 1979
Computing for Architects
  R A Reynolds
  Butterworth, London 1987

Magazine and periodicals

GENERAL
Architects' Journal
Building Design
Building

Bibliography

COMPUTING

Architects' Journal Information Technology Supplements
November 1987, April 1988, December 1988, June 1989
Building Design Supplement September 1988
    'Working Towards a Common System' by Richard Twinch

Business Computing
Byte
CICA Bulletin
Desktop Publishing Today
Micro Decision, in particular:
    'Designs on the Future' by Robert Piper, June/July 1989
PC Buyers Guide, in particular:
    'The Perils of PC Piper' by Robert Piper, June/July 1989
PC User
Personal Computer World, in particular:
    'On and Off the Record' by Duncan Campbell, October 1988
    'Less is More' by Colin Foster, April 1989
    'Mass Media' by Nick Hampshire, April 1989
Popular Computing Weekly
Practical Computing, in particular:
    'MAC v IBM' by Ian Stobie, Peter Jackson, November 1988;
    'Are Computers Bad for Your Health?' by Charles Christian, 'Injury Time'
    by Garret Keogh, 'Don't Let Power Drive You Crazy' by Samuel Dick, April
    1989
Systems International Graphics Extra
    Autumn 1988

Index